RUFUS JONES

MODERN SPIRITUAL MASTERS
Robert Ellsberg, Series Editor

This series introduces the writing and vision of some of the great spiritual masters of the twentieth century. Along with selections from their writings, each volume includes a comprehensive introduction, presenting the author's life and writings in context and drawing attention to points of special relevance to contemporary spirituality.

Some of these authors found a wide audience in their lifetimes. In other cases recognition has come long after their deaths. Some are rooted in long-established traditions of spirituality. Others charted new, untested paths. In each case, however, the authors in this series have engaged in a spiritual journey shaped by the influences and concerns of our age. Such concerns include the challenges of modern science, religious pluralism, secularism, and the quest for social justice.

At the dawn of a new millennium this series commends these modern spiritual masters, along with the saints and witnesses of previous centuries, as guides and companions to a new generation of seekers.

Already published:
Dietrich Bonhoeffer (edited by Robert Coles)
Simone Weil (edited by Eric O. Springsted)
Henri Nouwen (edited by Robert A. Jonas)
Pierre Teilhard de Chardin (edited by Ursula King)
Anthony de Mello (edited by William Dych, S.J.)
Charles de Foucauld (edited by Robert Ellsberg)
Oscar Romero (by Marie Dennis, Rennie Golden, and Scott Wright)
Eberhard Arnold (edited by Johann Christoph Arnold)
Thomas Merton (edited by Christine M. Bochen)
Thich Nhat Hahn (edited by Robert Ellsberg)

Forthcoming volumes include:
Flannery O'Connor
Edith Stein
G. K. Chesterton

MODERN SPIRITUAL MASTERS SERIES

RUFUS JONES

Essential Writings

Selected
with an Introduction by
KERRY WALTERS

ORBIS BOOKS
Maryknoll, New York 10545

The publisher gratefully acknowledges the permission of Mary Hoxie Jones and the Rufus M. Jones Trust to publish excerpts from the writings of Rufus Jones.

Library of Congress Cataloging-in-Publication Data
Jones, Rufus Matthew, 1863-1948.
    [Selections. 2001]
    Rufus Jones : essential writings / selected with an introduction by Kerry Walters.
        p.   cm. – (Modern spiritual masters series)
    Includes bibliographical references.
    ISBN 1-57075-380-6 (pbk.)
    1. Spiritual life. I. Walters, Kerry S. II. Title. III. Series.
BV4501.3 .J66 2001
248.4'896 – dc21

                                                    2001046176

For
Mary Hoxie Jones

Contents

Sources

Church   "The Church as an Organ of Social Ideals," in Jacques Maritain et al., *Religion and the Modern World: University of Pennsylvania Bicentennial Conference* (Philadelphia: University of Pennsylvania Press, 1941)

DF   *A Dynamic Faith* (London: Headley Brothers, 1906)

DS   *The Double Search: Studies in Atonement and Prayer* (Philadelphia: John C. Winston, 1906)

EG   *The Eternal Gospel* (New York: Macmillan, 1938)

FE   *Fundamental Ends of Life* (New York: Macmillan, 1925)

FP   *The Faith and Practice of Quakers* (London: Metheun, 1927)

FT   *Finding the Trail of Life* (New York: Macmillan, 1926)

IL   *The Inner Life* (New York: Macmillan, 1922)

MR   *Studies in Mystical Religion* (London: Macmillan, 1923)

NE   *New Eyes for Invisibles* (New York: Macmillan, 1943)

PC   *A Preface to Christian Faith in a New Age* (New York: Macmillan, 1932)

QS   *Quakerism and the Simple Life* (London: Headley
        Brothers, 1906)

RF   *Religious Foundations* (New York: Macmillan, 1923)

SE   *Spiritual Energies in Everyday Life* (New York:
        Macmillan, 1922)

SL   *Social Law in the Spiritual World: Studies in Human
        and Divine Inter-Relationship* (London: Swarthmore
        Press, 1923)

SM   *Spirit in Man* (Stanford: Stanford University Press,
        1941)

SP   *Some Problems of Life* (Nashville: Cokesbury, 1938)

TL   *The Trail of Life in the Middle Years* (New York:
        Macmillan, 1934)

TS   *The Testimony of the Soul* (New York: Macmillan,
        1937)

Why   "Why I Enroll with the Mystics," in *Contemporary
        American Theology: Theological Autobiographies*, ed.
        Vergilius Ferm (New York: Round Table Press, 1932)

Preface

Nobody knows how the kindling flame of life and power leaps from one life to another. What is the magic quality in a person which instantly awakens faith? You listen to a hundred persons unmoved and unchanged: you hear a few quiet words from the man with the kindling torch and you suddenly discover what life means for you forevermore.

Rufus Jones, Sermon at Trinity Church, Boston, 1932

My guess is that most of us would tremble with a sense of the uncanny if we took time to count up all the "happy accidents" or "lucky coincidences" that have transformed our lives. Despite our conceit of self-direction, we humans are frequently nudged onto unexpected pathways by events that suddenly drop from out of the blue — or from heaven, as the case may be. One of these transformative accidents in my own life was my discovery of Rufus Jones, the great twentieth-century Quaker mystic. Here's how it happened.

Although a member of the Woodstock generation, I was never a big rock-'n'-roll fan. For me, the only music worth listening to was jazz. So while my college classmates were turning onto the Stones or Pink Floyd, I was swaying to the rhythm of Lionel Hampton, Red Allen, Maynard Ferguson, Count Basie, and — first and always — the great Duke Ellington. My friends could never quite figure out what the attraction was. Still, the early 1970s was an aesthetically tolerant era, and we cheerfully agreed to disagree when it came to musical tastes.

But there *was* one thing my rock-'n'-roll friends and I agreed on: we liked percussion. In fact, we loved it. And so far as I was concerned at the time, the best jazz drummer around was a fellow sparkplugging for the Duke's band named Rufus "Speedy" Jones. Truth to tell, Speedy wasn't a first-class jazz drummer. He never made it big, and his passing in 1990 went mainly unnoticed. But he did play a few good solos in his time, and when Speedy Jones was good, he was absolutely explosive. He may not have been too subtle, but he sure was fun.

In 1973, at the height of my enthusiasm for Speedy's drumming, I was in my favorite used book store running an eye over the bargain table (twenty-five cents per book — a perfect price for an out-of-pocket college student). Then I saw it: a dark clothbound volume, ragged, dirty, and obviously a few years old. On the spine in faded gold letters I read: *A Call to What Is Vital*. The author was Rufus Jones.

My immediate assumption was that the book (improbable as this seemed) was by Speedy. After all, how many guys with a name like Rufus Jones could there possibly be? But some quick page-flipping showed me that the book was on religion — a subject I was enormously uninterested in at the time — and that it had been published back in 1948, when my Rufus Jones would have still been a kid. Still, it tickled me that this holy-roller author shared Speedy's name, and I had an extra quarter to spare. So I bought the book, took it back to my apartment, and lugged it around with my other possessions as I moved from place to place over the next few years. It was only in 1978, after I'd pretty much lost interest in Speedy Jones but was rapidly acquiring one in religion and spirituality, that I actually got around to reading it.

And when I did, a wonderful thing happened. I discovered that this other Rufus Jones was also a percussionist of sorts, a drummer-herald who sometimes softly, sometimes robustly, beat out a stirring song of God. Both Joneses stimulated my senses, the one with his wildly heady rhythm, the other with his elegantly moving prose. But the newly met Jones, the Quaker Jones, also thrilled my spirit. His drum roll told of a world ashimmer with the presence of a God who is as close to us as our own hearts, of a God who is experienced in the joys and sorrows of everyday life, of a God who is worshiped when we love and laugh and listen in expectant silence and share ourselves with others. In quick order this portly New England Quaker, who had died thirty years earlier, helped me begin to appreciate just how brilliantly all of existence is illuminated by the divine light. In such a magic-lantern world, surprises — happy accidents — are just around every corner.

I've been reading and thinking about Jones for over twenty years now, and I've grown increasingly convinced that his joyful celebration of God and service — reminiscent in so many ways of the message of an earlier troubadour of God, St. Francis of Assisi — is as timely as it ever was. His spirituality is optimistic without being pollyannish, commonsensical without falling into babbitry, and wise without being pretentious. It always reaches for harmonious vitality: the creative fusion of contemplative withdrawal and active stewardship, the in-flowing of the Divine into the quotidian, the birthing of the Heavenly Kingdom from the womb of the here-and-now world. These and other characteristic themes in Rufus Jones's thought ignited me two decades ago. In reading the selections collected here from his voluminous works, my hope is that you can discover for yourself that transformative "kindling flame of life" that sometimes leaps from one person to the next.

Although Jones's ideas and vision have aged well, his near-exclusive reliance upon masculine pronouns has not. The contemporary reader will probably find his use of "his," "he," "him," "man," and "mankind," when what he means is "their," "we," "us," "human," and "humankind," a bit unsettling. I, at least, do. But I've nonetheless decided to let Jones's original prose stand rather than attempt gender-neutral surgery on it that's bound to leave unseemly scars. In defense of Jones, I would plead two points: first, he wrote in the convention of his day, as do we all; second, despite his language, both he and his Quaker tradition are refreshingly nonsexist. This latter claim will, I trust, become evident in the selections that follow.

I'm very grateful to Robert Ellsberg of Orbis Books, my skilled and enthusiastic editor; to Diana Franzusoff Peterson, College Archivist, and Emma J. Lapsansky, Curator of Special Collections, Haverford College, for their generous legwork; to Matthew J. Walker, Mellon Bank, who ably represented the Rufus M. Jones Literary Trust; to Andreea Florescu, who proofread the original manuscript; and most of all to Mary Hoxie Jones, for her gracious permission to republish selections from her father's writings. This volume is dedicated to her.

I'm indebted to one other person as well. Thanks, Speedy.

Introduction

Mystic of the Everyday

*We do not know how far our own margins of being reach.
We cannot completely map the full area that properly belongs to us. No one can with certainty draw the boundary
between himself and the beyond himself, any more than
we can tell where the tidal river ends and the ocean begins,
but we unmistakably feel on occasions that tides from
beyond our own margins sweep into us and refresh us.*[1]

The American Friend Rufus Jones (1863–1948) was one of the
most beloved mystical writers of his generation — the *London
Times* went so far as to call him "the greatest spiritual philoso-
pher living in America" — but his name is not well known today
outside of Quaker circles. This is a pity, because Jones has much
wisdom to offer anyone who yearns for a richer interior life. His
message is especially timely in an age such as ours when God
seems remote if not downright absent to so many people. In
over fifty books and hundreds of essays and lectures, Jones as-
sured his audiences that God is very near indeed — that God, in
fact, dwells within every one of us as the "inner Light." We are
so inseparably connected to God that each of us, could we but
realize it, is permanently aglow with divine radiance. If we feel

15

cut off from God, it is we, not God, who have made ourselves absent.

At first glance, Jones's observation may not seem terribly original. On an abstract level, most of us probably agree with the theological doctrine of divine immanence, the claim that God is somehow in our midst even when we feel most abandoned. But giving an intellectual (and perhaps jaded) nod to the doctrine is not at all the same as *experiencing* and *living* its truth. The very ways we typically go about trying to find God suggest we haven't absorbed its full import. The upshot is that we often strain mightily but unwisely for God, and inflame rather than ease our deep restlessness.

Two good signs that we don't truly believe God is already present to us are our popular assumptions (1) that any genuine experience of God must be a flashy, road-to-Damascus encounter, and (2) that this lightning-bolt kind of epiphany is possible only by submitting to the spiritual equivalent of a boot camp obstacle course. Nothing less than skyrocketing ascents to beatific visions satisfies our sense of propriety, and we just assume that the only way to get off the launch pad is to subdue earthbound flesh with harshly ascetic or elaborately choreographed spiritual techniques. The more esoteric these techniques, the better. "Hidden" or "secret" wisdom is better rocket fuel than common sense.

But a couple of points are worth keeping in mind here. First, while it is true that mystical visions and ecstatic flights of the alone to the Alone are legitimate parts of the Christian spiritual tradition, it is also important to recall that all the great Christian teachers have cautioned against fixating on Hollywoodish special effects. (John of the Cross actually condemned the desire for them as a spiritual gluttony.) Our demand for pyrotechnics is based on the erroneous assumption that humans are so radically separated from God, either because of our own depravity or God's utter otherness, that the gulf can be bridged only by intense spiritual explosions that catapult us out of the everyday straight toward the divine core. To think in this way sets up a radically segregated universe where God hides away in his uptown penthouse and the rest of us get along as best we can in our downtown tenements. It goads us to despise everyday, concrete existence as a place of exile and to yearn for an ethereal spiritual realm that (we hope) is our "true" home.

The second point is this: while spiritual techniques can be helpful in preparing us to become increasingly open to God's presence in our lives, they are also terribly seductive. If we're not careful, we focus so intensely on our methods of seeking God that we become trapped in them. Fasting, prayer, meditation, *lectio divina,* contemplation, centering, controlled breathing, mantras, retreats, twelve-step programs: all these have value only if they are seen as disposable springboards to God. But because such techniques demand high levels of time and concentration from us, the sheer mastery of them can eventually mutate into an end in itself. When this happens, as the Buddhists are fond of saying, we confuse the finger and the moon, forgetting that the pointing finger is valuable only insofar as it directs our attention to the moon. A Zen story nicely illustrates this point. An eager young man goes to a great spiritual master. "I'm looking for enlightenment!" he announces. "If I become your disciple, how long will it take me to achieve it?" The old man shrugs. "Ten years, give or take." "Ten years?" exclaims the youngster. "That's way too long! I need to move faster than that! What if I work extra hard to subdue my flesh and learn all the spiritual exercises? How long will it take then?" "In that case," smiles the master, "we're looking at twenty, maybe thirty, years."

Rufus Jones offers a refreshing tonic against making the search for God more complicated than it need be. There are no esoteric secrets or magical incantations to be mastered, no life-denying training regimen to be endured. Instead, in keeping with Quakerism's traditional emphasis on simplicity, Jones teaches that the best "technique" is a full-hearted return to the everyday, Christlike life of the early Christians. (In this regard, he'd cheerfully concede that there's nothing "terribly original" about his thought.) The spirituality of the early church shimmered with celebratory awareness of the ongoing Incarnation, the here-and-now resplendence of the Divine. To its faithful, immanence was not just an arid theological doctrine; it was a living experience. God was visible — God was *present* — everywhere: in spring flowers and harvest-time grain, in the din of a crowded street and the silence of twilight, in churning waves and calm seas. But most of all, God was present in the deep-down core of each and every person.

For Jones, this means that the soul is inherently "conjunct" with God, inseparably linked to Spirit and thus by its very nature open to the Divine. There's no need for the distracting razzamatazz of esoteric techniques and visions and ecstasies, because God is already *here,* encountered in the everyday course of life or not at all. The good news is that *all* of us are budding "spiritual masters," entirely capable of the lovingly intimate experience of God that's traditionally been called "mystical" and reserved only for exemplary souls. Distinctions between the sacred and the everyday, the sacramental and the ordinary, break down. All creation sparkles with the presence of God, and "nothing now can be unimportant. There is more in the least event than the ordinary eye sees. Everywhere in the world there is stuff to be transmuted into divine material. Every situation may be turned into an occasion for winning a nearer view of God."[2]

God, in other words, is with us all along. The trick is opening one's eyes and looking.

•

Who was Rufus Jones? He unintentionally gives us a pretty good self-sketch in a passage he once wrote about Erasmus. In describing the great Renaissance leader, Jones could just as well have been describing himself:

> A Christian theologian who... undertook the task of saving Christianity from being submerged in arid debate and dogma, in subtleties and trivialities, and of restoring it once more to its true glory as a religion of life. He went back to the spirit and native power of the Gospel and took its exalted message seriously. He found the essential aspect of Christianity in the Sermon on the Mount. He longed to restore the ethical and spiritual depth of that primitive faith and vision of life. He abhorred war.... [H]e stood foursquare for a religion that would make, if it were taken seriously, a different man and a transformed society.[3]

The mystic who substituted a firsthand experience of God for theological "subtleties and trivialities"; the religious reformer who sought to restore "primitive faith and vision of life" to Christianity; the man of loving kindness who wished to integrate the "Gospel spirit" in general and the Sermon on the Mount in particular into his everyday life; the social prophet who "abhorred war" and strove for spiritual transformation at both the individual and the social levels: this was the American Friend Rufus Jones.

The boy who fathered the man was born on January 25, 1863, in the village of South China, Maine. His home was filled with the love, simplicity, and nurturing silence characteristic of pious Quaker households. It was there that young Rufus imbibed the gospel's deep message long before he ever read it for himself. "I was not christened in a church," he tells us, "but I was sprinkled from morning till night with the dew of religion. We never ate a meal which did not begin with a hush of thanksgiving; we never began a day without a 'family gathering' at which Mother read a chapter of the Bible, after which there would follow a weighty silence.... The life in our home was saturated with the reality and the practice of love. We spoke to each other as though love were ruling and guiding us."[4]

Particularly important in the youngster's life was the quiet influence of his paternal aunt, Peace Jones, whose holiness her nephew once likened to St. Francis of Assisi's. At Rufus's birth, Aunt Peace had taken him in her arms and made a prophecy: "This child will one day bear the message of the Gospel to distant lands and to peoples across the sea."[5] Her unassailable faith in his destiny, as well as her tender nursing, pulled him through a close brush with death when he was ten years old. A badly treated scratch on his foot led to blood poisoning that threatened first his leg and then his life. For nearly twelve months, Rufus was an invalid. The period forced him into precocious reflection and long conversations with Aunt Peace about God and life and death. This year of convalescence proved a turning point, drawing the youngster inward toward the Light at an age when most children are still preoccupied with games.

When Rufus recovered, he resumed the busy and boisterous life of a farm boy, helping his father with chores, attending the local school, and rejoining his friends in play and pranks. But his year of soul-searching convinced him that he wanted something more than village life. A scholarship took him to the Friends' Boarding School in Providence, Rhode Island, and in 1882 he entered Haverford College as a sophomore. During his three undergraduate years there, he immersed himself in the study of religion, philosophy, and history, eventually writing his senior thesis on mysticism. Upon graduation in 1885, he traveled in Europe, taught school for a year in New York, married and became a father, and served as headmaster of the Providence school where he'd once studied.

Then, in 1893, came another turning point in his life. He accepted an invitation to relocate to Philadelphia to become editor of *The Friends Review* and to teach at his alma mater. Agreeing to the editorship was a courageous decision. American Quakerism was in a bad way, torn between two competing factions. On the one hand, there were those Friends who remained loyal to Quakerism's gentle vision of an experiential faith based on receptive silence, simplicity, and service. On the other hand, there were those Friends who, inspired by the robust example of nineteenth-century evangelism, wished to transform Quakerism into a more institutionalized denomination, complete with pastors, fire-and-brimstone preaching, and biblical fundamentalism. This second group tended to be censorious of any activity it deemed "unscriptural" and regularly expelled Friends who, for example, dared to own pianos or read secular literature. The in-house squabbling between these two branches led, as one commentator put it, to a "pathetic deterioration of the Society — a process of cooling, hardening, stiffening, as lava once molten turns to rigid forms."[6]

In taking over the editorship of the *Review,* Jones aimed to heal the breach and at the same time restore Quakerism to its original emphasis on interior experience. He quickly merged the *Review* with a rival Chicago-based weekly, renamed it *The American Friend,* and announced his editorial pledge "to maintain and honor *spiritual realities* rather than *forms and traditions.*"[7] For the next twenty years, he consistently lived up to this vow. In hundreds of articles and editorials, Jones labored to end the bickering between liberal and conservative Quakers and to refocus their attention on what he took to be the heart of genuine religion: cultivation of openness to the inner Light, simplicity, and loving service to one's fellows. His conciliatory

approach angered many Friends and generated a good deal of
heated polemic on the part of detractors. It was not uncommon
for him to face hostile audiences when he spoke to Quakers
around the country. At one Midwestern Quaker college, for example, the president actually introduced Jones to students by
warning them that they would be listening to false doctrine and
should allow everything Jones said to go in one ear and out
the other. But by the time Jones stepped down as editor of *The
American Friend* in 1912, he'd gone a long way toward rec-
onciling his fellow Quakers and encouraging them to reexplore
their spiritual roots. He'd also made a name for himself in the
wider world as a religious author well worth heeding.

In addition to his demanding editorial work, Jones taught
philosophy, religion, and psychology at Haverford (from which
he retired only in 1933), wrote at least a book a year, regularly
visited Quakers in England and Europe, served on dozens of
boards and committees, crisscrossed the country giving talks to
Quakers and non-Quakers alike on mysticism and the spiritual
life, and somehow found time to earn an advanced degree in
philosophy from Harvard. It was a regimen that would have
killed a different man, and at times it took a heavy toll on
Jones's emotional and physical health. But he was sustained by
his conviction that "being and doing" were as important as
"writing and thinking." For Jones, as for the early Christians
to whose example he looked, there was no conflict between his
own deeply mystical temperament and his busy life as editor,
author, teacher, and critic. Both were means to one and the
same end: honoring God. As the seventeenth-century Quaker
William Penn wrote, "True godliness does not turn men out of
the world, but enables them to live better in it and excites their
endeavors to mend it."

In the midst of all this activity, a third and dreadful turning
point occurred in Jones's life: his wife, Sarah, died of tuberculo-

sis in 1899, and their son, Lowell, on whom Jones doted, died a short four years later of diphtheria. Both deaths hit Jones hard, but they also helped him grapple in a fruitful way with his core conviction that there was a deep, underlying meaning to such tragic events. Lowell's death in particular pushed Jones to this conclusion by sparking one of his most memorable mystical experiences (his description of it, as well as of two other mystical episodes, is included in this volume's "Overture"). Jones later remarried and lived happily with his second wife, Elizabeth Bartram Cadbury, and daughter, Mary Hoxie, for almost half a century. But he mourned this early loss for the rest of his days. Some of his tenderest prose was written reminiscing about Lowell.

A fourth period in Jones's life and work began in 1917 with the founding of the American Friends Service Committee (AFSC), a relief organization that embodied Quakerism's gospel-based resistance to violence and injustice. Jones had long been involved in efforts to improve conditions for the poor, the ill, and the imprisoned, but his commitment to these causes doubled in his last three decades. He considered his piloting of the AFSC through both world wars his single most important achievement. Originally organized to provide conscientious objectors with a peaceful alternative to combat service during World War I, the AFSC quickly became an important source of economic and humanitarian relief for war-torn or economically ravaged countries across the globe. When the AFSC was awarded the Nobel Peace Prize in 1947, it was largely because Rufus Jones had steered the organization so wisely for thirty-odd years.

Jones's work with the AFSC took him to many countries in his later years. In addition, he traveled extensively in Asia, India, and Africa, teaching and lecturing as he went. (On one of these trips he meet Mohandas Gandhi. The two were immea-

surably impressed with each other.) Shortly before the outbreak
of World War II, Jones even sailed to Nazi Germany to intervene on behalf of the Jews. Although he met with several
high-ranking Gestapo officials, his efforts obviously proved un-
successful. But the very fact that he undertook such a mission
while in his late seventies attests to his earnest willingness to
sacrifice comfort and even personal well-being for the sake of
the gospel. As a young man he'd written: "I believe more and
more that the greatest single help to a spiritual life is a deep
and living human love for another. . . . I have solemnly resolved
to love more deeply and more truly and to be a sweeter man."[8]
Unlike the resolutions of many young men, this one was carried through with remarkable consistency throughout a very
long life.

When Rufus Jones died at his summer home in South China,
Maine, on June 16, 1948, shortly after correcting the proofs of
his last book, he was mourned by tens of thousands of people
all over the world. In their eyes, he was one of the greatest
spiritual masters of his day. His own appraisal of his life was
more modest. He once wrote, "I assume that the major business we are here for in this world is to be a rightly fashioned
person as an organ of the divine purpose."[9] So far as Jones was
concerned, all he'd done was go about his Father's business.

•

Rufus Jones's spirituality has deep Quaker roots. So before we
explore his own thought, it may be helpful to say a few words
about its context.

The Religious Society of Friends was born in mid-seventeenth-
century England. Partly a response to Puritanism's gloomy
worldview, but mainly a charismatic reawakening to the in-
dwelling presence of God (variously referred to as the "Light of
Christ," the "inward Christ," the "Root," the "Principle," the

"Spirit," the "Seed," and the "inner Light"), Quakerism preached a back-to-basics spirituality. The movement's founder, George Fox (1624–91), taught that tortuous theology and elaborate ecclesial structures are impediments to the "inward quickenings," or divine inspirations, emphasized by the early church. Nothing artificial should intervene between the yearning heart and God. All that's truly required for salvation is a humble and loving resolve to so heed and conform to the "inner Light" that any dissonance between self-will and divine will evaporates. As Fox's friend Isaac Penington (1616–79) put it, "It is not enough to hear of Christ, or read of Christ; but this is the thing, to feel him my root, my life, my foundation; and my soul engrafted into him, by him who hath power to engraft."

From the very beginning, then, Quakerism was radically democratic in its conviction that every person is capable of personally experiencing God, and deeply suspicious that mere theological abstractions get in the way of either an immediate encounter with God or a humble imitation of Christ's compassion and love. It sought to recover the uncluttered simplicity of primitive Christianity, and its primary way of doing this was to insist that a personal experience of the inner Light was the true source of genuine religion. As Jones himself summed it up, "The whole significance of the Quaker movement was its revolt from theories and notions and its appeal instead to experience."[10] True, Quakers sometimes disagreed about whether the inner Light was an innate aspect of the human soul or a blessing subsequently bestowed on fallen humans by a gracious God. But all of them accepted it as their starting point, citing biblical passages that, for example, call Jesus "the true light, which enlightens everyone" (John 1:9), claim that God's Spirit will come and guide humans into truth (John 16:13), or remind us that we have within us the "imperishable seed" of God's "living and enduring word" (1 Pet. 1:23). The essential Quaker belief, as George Fox put it, is that "Christ has already come and doth dwell in the hearts of his people," and it was a belief based on scriptural authority as well as personal experience. Over time, this emphasis on the inner Light set a distinctive stamp on Quaker spirituality. Silent receptivity to the inner Light, private prayer and corporate forms of meditation that invite forth revelatory "openings," obedient conformity of one's will to those openings, apostolic simplicity in living, seeing God in all things, joyful service to others in imitation of Christ, an unswerving fidelity to pacifism, toleration in matters of conscience: these became staples of the Quaker way. Rufus Jones imbibed them as a youngster in South China, Maine. They were the foundations of his own mysticism and ministry.

And of his theology, too. Jones agreed with his fellow Quakers that overintellectualizing faith is a mistake, and that at the end of the day we must bow in silent awe before the divine mystery. But he parted company with his more quietistic coreligionists in his conviction that it was still important to reflect deeply and prayerfully on what the experience of the inner Light reveals about God and the human condition.

One of Jones's favorite stories had to do with a youthful visit he paid to a Friends' meeting house in Birmingham, England. The traditional Quaker worship practice was (and is) to conduct meeting in silence, with the understanding that any person who felt the inner Light prompting him or her to speak could do so. Jones tells us that after a little while he rose to say a few words, prefacing his nervous remarks with: "Since sitting in this meeting I have been thinking...." Afterwards, one of the elders took him aside. "I was grieved at what thou said in meeting," he told Jones. "Thou said that since sitting in meeting thou hadst been thinking. Thou shouldst *not* have been thinking."

One reason Jones so enjoyed this story is because it emphasizes the importance traditional Quakerism places on silent openness to the inner Light. But he also liked telling it because it poked gentle fun at the attitude, all too common in his youth, that *any* "thinking" about God, whether in or out of meeting, was somehow inappropriate. This is a position Jones could never accept. Starting with his Haverford senior thesis on mysticism and continuing in his journalism, books, lectures, and sermons, he always worked under the assumption that a great deal more can be said about God and the Christian life than popular piety might allow. He remained intensely loyal to his Quaker background. But like the prophet he was, he pushed forward to explore new spiritual territory and encouraged the rest of us, Quaker and non-Quaker alike, to share the adventure with him.

•

Not surprisingly, the starting point for all of Jones's religious writing is the lived experience of the inner Light. Personal experience, scriptural authority, and the testimony of countless believers convinced him that the inner Light — or, as he generally called it, "the Beyond within" or "the More" — is an undeniable reality. Given that certainty, the questions that most intrigued him centered around what the inner Light experience can reveal about (1) the nature of reality, (2) the possibility of mystical communion with God, (3) the destiny of humanity, and (4) proper action in the world. Jones's sixty-year exploration of these matters is sampled in this volume, but a few general words about his conclusions are in order here.

1. What can the inner Light experience tell us about reality? The most obvious inference to be drawn is that reality must be such that it allows a "mutual and reciprocal correspondence" between God and humans. This phrase, borrowed from Clement of Alexandria, was Jones's shorthand expression for his abiding conviction that the universe is so deeply imbued

with God's presence that we inevitably come into contact with a *spiritual* "over-world" whenever we think deeply about the *material* world around us. This over-world, intuited in our experiences of beauty, truth, love, and goodness — all of which imbue physicality without being reducible to physical explanations or categories — permeates the natural order of things. As the Jesuit poet Gerard Manley Hopkins would have said, the over-world is the "inscape" or deep-down spiritual essence of everything that is. For Jones, the inscaped Spirit that flows through the material world is nothing less than the ongoing incarnational presence of God.

Obviously the incarnation extends from the natural to the human realm. The very fact that humans are capable of picking up on traces of the spiritual over-world in experiences of beauty or love suggests that we ourselves must have some affinity to it. After all, like knows like. So Jones concludes that the same Spirit running through the world of nature likewise percolates through us. We carry a spark of the Divine within our deepest core — God's being "opens into ours, and ours into His" — and we have only to rest our heads upon our breasts to notice it.[11]

The abiding presence of God in creation renders all reality holy. Because it is deeply interfused with Spirit, the universe in which we dwell is sacramental and ought to be cherished as the outward and visible symbol of God it is. This sacramental holiness wonderfully extends to the human soul as well. Contrary to Augustinian attempts to paint the soul as utterly depraved through original sin, Jones strongly denies that anything as essentially conjunct to God as the soul can be evil. Still, he's no naïve optimist when it comes to either humans or nature. He knows too well that individual persons are capable of great wickedness, and that nature "red in tooth and claw" often appears indifferent if not outright hostile to human welfare. But the first problem is fixable through the power of transformative love, and the second ameliorable, at least in part, through God-given reason.

2. So much for what the inner Light can tell us about reality. What about the possibility of mystical connection with God? Jones's answer to this question is perhaps his single most distinctive contribution as a spiritual writer. His insights are based not only on his lifelong study of mystical literature, but also on his own mystical experiences.

The very fact that the soul is conjunct to God implies that humans possess a preapprehension of the Divine that lies behind all our perceptions of the world and conceptions about its structure. Without this preapprehension, we would be incapable of knowing either the world or, for that matter, God. As Jones points out, "If God could not and did not have a witness to Himself within our spirits, it is difficult to see how we could ever expect to establish the reality of His being."[12] The goal of the spiritual life is to bring this innate but frequently inarticulate preapprehension of God to the forefront of one's aware experience. Only then, when we consciously discover our ability to see "essential realities," are we capable of entering into that immediate relationship with God that Jones takes to be the hallmark of mysticism.

But how to go about cultivating new eyes with which to see essential realities? One tradition in Christian mysticism has it that spiritual clarity is a matter of drastically reducing the field of vision. The person who longs for direct experience of God must move away from everything that *is not* God: the outer physical world as well as the inner intellectual and emotional one. The goal is to negate any and all finite distractions until awareness, as Jones describes it, "becomes absorbed in God — swallowed up in the Godhead."[13] Only then is direct contact with the deity possible. Since such a total negation of self-consciousness is extremely difficult to achieve, this tradition places a high premium on spiritual exercises and techniques that claim to train us in mystical sensitivity, and is quite taken with "ecstasies" or "visions" in which mystics lose themselves.

Jones does not deny that this approach, generally called "negative" or "apophatic" mysticism, is possible for "rare" souls such as a Pseudo-Dionysius or a Teresa of Avila. But he does insist that it should not be held up as the normative ideal for the rest of us. Most people simply are not capable of blotting out consciousness of the self and the world to reach such heights, and to teach that the "all or nothing" apophatic way is the only mystical route to God is to set them up for needless spiritual alienation. A more common approach — and one, Jones believes, that's more compatible with the teachings and practice of the early church — is what he calls "affirmation," "practical," or sometimes "conative" mysticism. It is the mysticism of everyday life.

In contrast to the apophatic way, affirmation mysticism takes as its starting point the assumption that an immediate experience of God *can* be attained through the finite. This only makes sense, given Jones's conviction that the universe shimmers with the presence of the incarnate God and that the human spirit is inseparably conjunct with Spirit. Finite creation, in all its rich diversity, should be celebrated as the divine mirror of Infinity it is. The point is not to flee the everyday, deploring it as an obstacle to mystical fellowship with God, but rather to grow sensitive to the many "openings" it offers. Nor need self-awareness be negated in order to achieve mystical communion with God. Mystical union, according to Jones, is not an *erasure* of self so much as its transfigurative *awakening* to its inherent God-likeness. For Jones, Jesus is the prototypical mystic: a person who discovered his true self because he lived in utter harmony with the Father. His personality is not negated by mystical contact with God. On the contrary, it is completed, brought to fulfillment, such that "we see at last in him what man was meant to be — as we usually have not done — the divine possibilities of the human nature we bear."[14]

Jones wrote about affirmative mysticism in book after book, boring into it from different angles, continuously refining his analysis, searching for new ways to present the liberating news that God can be intimately experienced in the course of everyday living, that the Infinite is discernible in and through the finite, and that our enfleshed existence in the world is to be celebrated rather than punished by misguided life-denying ascetic techniques. In this regard, his mysticism is reminiscent of Francis of Assisi's rapturously sensual joy in nature, Brother Lawrence's tranquil practice of the presence of God, or Thérèse de Lisieux's discernment of God in the little things of life.

3. Jones's belief that mysticism properly fulfills rather than negates the self directly connects with his understanding of human destiny. The end for which we are created — the end toward which the inner Light continuously draws us — is self-aware membership in the Body of Christ and creative partnership in the Kingdom of Heaven, that beloved community in which God's cosmic plan reaches fruition.

The doctrine of the Body of Christ is crucial to Jones's spirituality. As a Quaker, he always puts a high premium on fellowship. For him, the "primary fact of human life is the group," not the ruggedly stand-alone individual.[15] Even though mystical communion with God is experienced by the individual worshiper, its deeper meaning rests on the entire family of believers — the Church. The "Church," then, is more than just a socially constructed or historical institution. More fundamentally, it is the living expression and growing interpretation, here and now, in the midst of the finite, of Christ's eternal mind and infinite spirit and message — an expression and interpretation that binds all believers together into one "Body." The outer, visible church, in fact, has meaning and value only insofar as it functions as a visible expression of the underlying mystical Body.

Jones, like St. Paul before him, takes this notion of *body* seriously. For him, the community of all believers truly is a spiritual organism in which the parts, or "cells" are intimately related to the whole and the well-being of each member dependent on the health of others. Like all organisms, the Body of Christ is called to grow and flourish. The energy that animates this growth is love, because love is "the principle of the spiritual universe, as gravitation is of the physical."[16] The better we members of the Body love, the more Christlike or "alive" we become, thereby reaffirming the great gift of being God has bestowed upon us. Jones strikingly calls this joyful affirmation of existence "living to live" — living so fully that any deathlike separation from God brought about by sin is overcome. In addition, the more Christlike we grow, the better we nurture the growth of our neighbors. Held together by the "inner gravitation" of love, the spiritual organism of which we are parts pulsates with vitality.

As members of the Body of Christ, forever bound by the inner Light to God and to one another, we are blessed with a great and awesome task: cooperating with God to bring about the Heavenly Kingdom. The incarnational God works through us, using our hearts and minds and bodies as vehicles of divine will and renewal in the world. Attuning more closely to the inner Light, each of us grows increasingly aware of personal gifts and talents that might be used to extend the presence of the living Lord throughout the entire world. Growing in self-knowledge and love, we comport ourselves in ways that bring humanity, and indeed all of creation, closer to the promised Kingdom. The Kingdom, Jones assures us, *will* come, in spite of the fact that it often seems woefully distant. But it is not a gift that will be handed to us so much as a "present task" to which all members of the Body of Christ are called. Its advent will be by little and by little, built upon our willingness to "go the second mile" with acts of love, compassion, and kindness.

4. And what are these acts of love? This, the final concern raised by the inner Light experience, is central for Jones because he believes that genuine mystical religion always leads to good works in the world. Christianity, as George Fox insisted time and again, is never merely "notional." Mystical union with the incarnate God, far from separating us from daily life, situates us squarely in the world. How could it be otherwise for worshipers of an Infinite God who self-reveals in the finite? Consequently, "there is no inner life that is not also an outer life. To withdraw from the stress and strain of practical action and from the complication of problems into the quiet cell of the inner life in order to build its domain undisturbed is the sure way to lose the inner life." God is love, and love is impelled by its own logic to reach out and build up: "Religion does not consist of inward thrills and private enjoyment of God; it does not terminate in beatific vision. It is rather the joyous business of carrying the Life of God into the lives of men — of being to the eternal God what a man's hand is to a man."[17]

The loving acts we are called to perform certainly are not world-shaking deeds of valor and heroism, or at least they need not be. Instead, in keeping with Jones's insistence that the extraordinary is found in the ordinary, they are the "commonplace" activities that fill the days of our lives. The secret is not in *what* one does so much as in *how* one does it. A life attuned to the inner Light and in love with God and creation inevitably makes a difference in the world, transforming the most mundane act into a holy and celebratory rite whose effects ripple outwardly.

One work of love that helps build the Kingdom is prayer, the intentional effort to open ourselves ever more deeply to the inner Light. Jones is careful to point out that prayer is not a wordy affair of magical incantation or desperate, self-centered pleading. At its best, prayer is a silent and loving communion of spirit with Spirit. It's very much like the openness we display when we're around a very good friend: we need not continuously chatter to be closely connected. The analogy to friendship is important here, because Jones believes that genuine prayer is neither a spiritual nor psychological possibility unless it is mediated through the concrete person of Jesus Christ. We do not — we cannot — pray to an abstract Infinite. Instead, prayer is based on "live faith in an Infinite Person who is corporate with our lives."[18] Prayer, in other words, emerges from the Body of Christ and directs itself to the living Christ.

Cultivation of the spirit of simplicity — the blessing Jesus referred to as inner poverty — is another work of love that actively builds God's Kingdom. Jones contrasts this spirit with what he calls "commercialism." The heart of simplicity is honest recognition and acceptance of what's real, true, important. The simple person refuses to be either bamboozled or seduced by the religious, economic, intellectual, and political frills and fashions that our "commercialist" society pretends are realities. This simplicity of spirit allows for the discovery that just *being* — living to live, as Jones would say — is much more fundamental than *having*. At its very heart, then, simplicity is an attunement to the wonder of existence, and a profound appreciation of the liberatingly audacious fact that we *are*. Living simply in the world frees us from the manic urge to acquire possessions — be they religious dogmas, political power, media prestige, or material wealth — while at the same time also freeing us to *be* for others and for God.

The spirit of simplicity liberates us to love the world and its people, and such love clearly demands humble toleration — or, better, loving acceptance — of religious pluralism. Jones believes

there are as many legitimate paths to God as there are individu-
als — the inner Light works with the raw material it is given —
and he deplores the dogmatism that condemns any religious approach or tradition simply because it is "different." To trust in
the inner Light is to find the courage to experiment with life
and to encourage others to do so as well. After all, cells within
the spiritual organism need growing room if they are to thrive;
unity, not uniformity, is the ideal. Loving acceptance provides
this room, creating the safe space to envision and entertain new
possibilities, including the most radical and at the same time the
most scriptural one of them all: peace. Put in a slightly different way, acceptance is an act of love that frees us to cooperate
with one another and with God so that the highest ideals of the
Christian ethos might become actual. Acceptance is also an expression of simplicity, because it is a humble recognition that
no single "ism" (least of all one's own!) holds a monopoly on
truth. Finally, acceptance is closely akin to prayer in that both
emerge from a radical openness to the other.

•

At the beginning of these introductory remarks, I told the Zen
story of the young would-be disciple looking for a fast track to
God and enlightenment. I'd like to finish with another tale, one
from the Sufi tradition. Rufus Jones always loved a good story.
I think he would have particularly enjoyed this one.

It seems that a certain man was frantically scratching around
in the sand outside his front door when a neighbor walked
by. "Abdullah my friend," the neighbor said. "Whatever are
you looking for?" "My treasure!" cried the distraught Abdullah. "I've lost my treasure!" "Well, calm yourself," replied
the neighbor. "I'll help you look for it. With the two of us
searching, and with Allah's help, we'll find it in no time."

So the two men squatted down side-by-side in the scorching

sun for the next four hours, combing through the sand in search of the lost treasure. Finally the neighbor, exhausted and near fainting from the heat, had enough. "Abdullah," he gasped, "I grow weary. We've looked and looked, and found nothing. Are you *sure* this is where you lost your treasure?"

"What are you talking about?" snapped the equally exhausted Abdullah. "I never said I lost it *here!* I lost it somewhere inside my *house.*"

"Then why in the name of all that's holy are we looking out *here!*" cried his exasperated neighbor.

"Because it's lighter out here than inside, of course!"

This funny little parable captures the spirit of Rufus Jones's central message to us: that frequently we too are Abdullahs, searching for God — our treasure — in all the wrong places. We assume that God can be found only in ecstatic moments of consumingly brilliant light that take us far from our "homes," the concrete existences in which we dwell. So we foolishly refuse to look in the nooks and crannies of our everyday lives because we fancy they are too drably mundane to hold God. But it is precisely there, in our homes, in the finite activities and the quite ordinary persons who surround us, that God can be found. The commonplace shimmers with depth, with naked, unfiltered Reality, and the everyday mysticism practiced and taught by Rufus Jones seeks to remind us of this great and joyful truth. God is with us always, because God is *here, now*, in the world. This is what the first Christians so vividly experienced. Our problem is that we've lost their sensitivity.

> We of the modern time live much more in the attitude of interrogation than of exclamation. We so blur our world with question marks that we lose the sense of wonder and sometimes even of vision. It is refreshing to note how frequently the great spiritual teachers of the New Testament

introduce their message with the word "behold!" They speak because they see and they want their hearers and their readers to see. Their "behold" is more than an interjection — it has the force of an imperative, as though they would say: "Just see what I see. Open your eyes to the full meaning of what is before you," which is the method of all true teachers.[19]

Learning once more to behold the inner Light: this is a simple task — as all spiritual imperatives are — but at the same time the greatest of all tasks. Rufus Jones was a man who *had* learned. His wonderful gift to us is his counsel to open our own eyes, in wonder and gratitude and awe, to the full meaning of what's always before us.

NOTES

1. Rufus Jones, *Pathways to the Reality of God* (New York: Macmillan, 1931), 199.

2. Rufus Jones, *Social Law in the Spiritual World: Studies in Human and Divine Inter-Relationship* (London: Swarthmore Press, 1923), 136.

3. Rufus Jones, *The Luminous Trail* (New York: Macmillan, 1947), 98.

4. Rufus Jones, *A Small-Town Boy* (New York: Macmillan, 1941), 32.

5. Rufus Jones, *Finding the Trail of Life* (New York: Macmillan, 1926), 20.

6. Harry Emerson Fosdick, *Rufus Jones Speaks to Our Time* (New York: Macmillan, 1951), ix.

7. Rufus Jones, *The Trail of Life in the Middle Years* (New York: Macmillan, 1934), 36.

8. Elizabeth Gray Vining, *Friend of Life: A Biography of Rufus Jones* (Philadelphia Yearly Meeting of the Religious Society of Friends, 1981), 72, 137. These are excerpts from two different letters written by Jones.

9. Rufus Jones, *The Luminous Trail*, 13.

10. Rufus Jones, ed., *Religious Foundations* (New York: Macmillan, 1923), 36.

11. Rufus Jones, *The Double Search: Studies in Atonement and Prayer* (Philadelphia: John C. Winston, 1906), 100.

12. Rufus Jones, *A Dynamic Faith*, 3d ed. (London: Headley Brothers, 1906), 3.

13. Rufus Jones, *Social Law in the Spiritual World*, 132.

14. Rufus Jones, *A Call to What Is Vital* (New York: Macmillan, 1948), 109–10.

15. Rufus Jones, "The Church as an Organ of Social Ideals," in Jacques Maritain et al., *Religion and the Modern World: University of Pennsylvania Bicentennial Conference* (Philadelphia: University of Pennsylvania Press, 1941), 110.

16. Rufus Jones, *The Double Search*, 110.

17. Rufus Jones, *The Inner Life* (New York: Macmillan, 1922), v, vi.

18. Rufus Jones, *The Double Search*, 107.

19. Mary Hoxie Jones, ed., *Thou Dost Open Up My Life* (Wallingford, Pa.: Pendle Hill Publications, 1973), 22. The excerpt is from a sermon Jones delivered at Harvard sometime in the late 1920s.

Overture

Rufus Jones wrote several autobiographical volumes during his lifetime. But the single most revealing memoir he left was a short essay published in his seventieth year. In it, Jones gives some idea of his own deep-seated mystical sensibility. He also provides us with a short statement of his religious teachings. Taken together, these two excerpts offer us an excellent entrée into his thought and spirituality.

WHY I ENROLL
WITH THE MYSTICS

I was born with a large strain of Celtic stock and my racial inheritance links me up with the men who in the dim past went on eager quests for the Holy Grail. That spirit of quest is as much a part of my elemental nature as is the color of my eyes and hair. It was a force to be reckoned with as soon as I began to live. I have never been able to confine my interests or my activities to things in space. I was the kind of child that had no more difficulty in seeing Jacob's ladders going up from earth to heaven than I had in seeing where the best apples grew. Wordsworth might have been writing of my cradle when he said:

A child more than all other gifts
That earth can offer to declining man
Brings hope with it, and forward looking thoughts.

The environment into which I came ministered in happy harmony to the natural bent of disposition. The beauty of the lake
on whose shores I lived, the mystery of distant mountains seen
on days of good visibility, the lure of the surrounding forests,
rich in the suggestions of the unexplored, quickened my imagination and fed the poetic side of my nature. But by far the most
important factor was the unnamed and unconscious mystical
propensity of my family. The word "mystical" was never spoken and of course had never been heard in our circle. It was
implicit practice and not explicit theory that counted. I was
immersed in a group mystical life from the very birth of consciousness and memory. Every day after breakfast we had a
long period of family silent worship, during which all the older
members of the group seemed to be plainly communing in joyous fellowship with a real Presence. The reality of it all was so
great, and the certainty of something more than just ourselves
in the room was so clearly felt that we little folks were caught
into the experience and carried along with the others. The mysterious hush had its own awe and the rapt look on the older
faces deepened the sense of awe and wonder. By the time I was
four years old I had formed the habit of using corporate silence
in a heightening and effective way. It brought with it, even for
the child, a sense of Presence.

Not much later than that early period of four I began to be
taken to Quaker meeting for worship. It involved a ride of three
miles through marvelous woods, which even now stir me with
indescribable emotions, and that was a moving preparation for
the main event. We sat together nearly two hours, a large part
of the time in silence. Some of the speaking was marked by

unmistakable inspiration, for two of the leading Quakers in America [Jones's aunt and uncle, Sybil and Eli Jones] belonged in that group, and some of it was extremely "dull," when it was not "queer," as it often was. But once more there was something contagious about the silence. It caught us all into its living fold. The persons who composed the group were, for the most part, simple, rustic people who came from their farms and their kitchens, but one felt that they knew God and found Him there. There was a touch of awe and majesty, of surprise and wonder, and while there was very little "thinking," or "thought-content," there was a gleam of eternal reality breaking on the humble group which put a kind of spell on the little boy in the midst.

The major spiritual influence in my early youth was from a refined and saintly maiden aunt who lived in our somewhat patriarchal and expansive home. She possessed quite unusual spiritual gifts and qualities of life. She had, to a rare degree, brought herself into parallelism with divine currents and she was extraordinarily sensitive to the environment of the Spirit. She seemed by swift intuition to know what the will of God was for almost every occasion of life. She *saw* what she ought to do with vividness and clarity. In periods of silent communion her face was radiant and she appeared to be having direct intercourse with a great Companion. She had frequent insights, or "openings," as to my course of life and I became impressed very early that she knew everything about me. There was never any use trying to conceal anything from her, for in all the deeper matters of life she read me like an open book. But with all her desire to guide me her grace and sweetness were so amazing that she left me wholly free to follow my own conscience and to walk my own path of life without constraint. . . . It was here in Aunt Peace that I first learned of the might of gentle forces. She was a Franciscan type of person, without, in fact, knowing anything of "God's poor little man" of Assisi. She always conquered and governed by soul-force, by grace and gentleness, quiet persuasion and the pull of attractive power. She wore the armor of light and her weapons were radiant forces.

— Why 191–93, 194

The "unnamed and unconscious mystical propensity of my family" remained with Jones his entire life. He frequently sensed God's presence in both private and communal prayer, feeling himself drawn into an intimate fellowship with the Divine which he interpreted as the essence of mysticism. Three experiences of "quiet mystical receptivity" in particular struck him as life-changing. The first occurred in 1892 while Jones was hiking in the Alps; the second in 1902, when his son, Lowell, died; and the third on Thanksgiving Day in 1922, when he was struck and almost killed by an automobile.

Once at sea, in the middle of the night, when all unknown to me my little boy, left behind in America, was dying with no father by him to hold his hand, I suddenly felt myself surrounded by an enfolding Presence and held as though by invisible Arms. My entire being was fortified and I was inwardly prepared to meet the message of sorrow which was awaiting me next day at the dock.

Another experience came much earlier in my life when I was spending a year abroad after graduation from college. It was at Dieu-le-fit in France, near the foothills of the Alps. I was walking alone in a forest, trying to map out my plan of life and confronted with issues which seemed too complex and difficult for my mind to solve. Suddenly I felt the walls between the visible and the invisible grow thin and the Eternal seemed to break through into the world where I was. I saw no flood of light, I heard no voice, but I felt as though I were face to face with a higher order of reality than that of the trees or mountains. I went down on my knees there in the woods with that same feeling of awe which compelled men in earlier times to take off their shoes from their feet. A sense of mission broke in on me and I felt that I was being called to a well-defined task of life to which I then and there dedicated myself. There have been other similar occasions, though none quite so overbrimming or charged to the same degree with the conviction of objective reality as these two which I have given. There was no excitement, no unusual emotion, no trance or ecstasy. But in both instances there was an emergence of power and fortification. I was brought to a new level of life and have never quite lost the transforming effect of the experience....

I have been present in many gatherings where this has happened and these occasions have confirmed and strengthened my faith and expectation that God is near at hand. Genuine worship of the highest type feels like "divine mutual and reciprocal correspondence." It is a two-way communion and not merely a one-sided effort. The way of worship has been well called "the way of wonder." It is an overbrimming experience by which life is made buoyant and triumphant and one is surprised that this greatest of all fine arts of life is so little used and practiced.

Another experience of a different type should perhaps be related. This time there was no single moment of invasion or of uprush. I discovered that a new life and power had come to me without my knowing precisely when it came. I was hit by an automobile one night while away from home. It happened without any preparation for it. No sound, no light, no consciousness of danger, preceded the startling event. Suddenly I felt my chest break and cave in. At the same time there was a powerful impact on my leg and then my body was hurled through space with tremendous force. The odd thing was that I did no thinking. I just *felt*. I was vaguely aware that an irresistible force was crushing the life out of my body, but I had no touch of fear. There was a huge boulder of undifferentiated experience, undisturbed by reflection and without the emergence of any overwhelming emotions. I was as near neighbor to death as I shall ever be while actually living, as close to the border of our world here as one ever can be and return again to the fullness of life, and yet there was not the least sense of fear or terror. When the doctor arrived a few minutes after the accident, my heart was beating regularly and my pulse was normal. In a few days I was brought home, carried to my spacious library and settled into a high modern hospital bed. I was strapped tight to protect my broken ribs. My leg was fastened in a fracture case so that I could not turn, for the slightest movement hurt me. My students brought moveable chairs, filling the room, and I went on with my college lectures, and finished all my courses, lying thus flat on my back, feeling all the time an unusual élan. Gradually I began to discover the amazing power of regeneration which living tissue reveals. Forces as gentle as the fall of snow flakes began to operate as though miracles had not ceased. The split and broken bones were woven together again. The ligaments were stretched back and fastened in their old places. The lacerated muscles were healed by some hidden alchemy. The torn skin and contused flesh were made whole by unseen processes. Every broken fiber was regenerated as though nature's whole business were restoration and renewal.

It was a long time before I realized that a still deeper miracle had been taking place within me. I cannot quite date the discovery. But it began to dawn upon me that a "restoration" of another sort had gone on. I seemed in a new way to be liberated from fears and anxieties and worries. I had entered into an unexpected tranquility and peace. More than that I had gained an immense increase of vitality and *vis viva*. Life had become a more joyous and radiant affair than I had ever known. I no longer cared anything about arguments to prove the reality of God, any more than I did to prove the incomparable worth of the human love which surrounded my life as I lay quietly recovering. I do not know how I reached the new level of conviction or how I got from one stage of life to the higher one on which I found myself. It has always seemed to me to be a case of quiet mystical receptivity. Spiritual energies of a more or less permanent order flowed in and operated, as though God at my fountains far off had been raining. The infallible-minded psychologists can no doubt easily explain it by naturalistic processes, but to one who has lived through it and lived in it and not yet outlived it, it seems too rich and wonderful and eternally good to be just the flushing of a gland! A learned man could give it a clumsy name, but when all is said such things can be truly appreciated and appraised only from within. — Why 206–9

CREDO

There is a Beyond, a More yet, within us, and it appears to be akin to us. We are finite-infinite and temporal-eternal beings in our very constitution. We are what we are and we partake of More in ideal and upward directions. There is a central rational-Spiritual nucleus in us which could have no other adequate origin than from the Spiritual Deeps of a World-Mind, or World-Reason out of which we emerged into individual form and struck our being into personal bounds. The ultimate Reality of the universe seems to be more nearly like us as we essentially are in our inmost nature than like anything else of which we know. But we possess rather tragic limitations in our unique and differentiated form as persons, though we appear to be morally autonomous and capable of imperial expansion through realization of our inherent possibilities. At our best we seem to be inwardly *conjunct* with the Life that is our Source. We find ourselves in intimate reciprocal relations with the ultimate Spiritual Reality of the universe and we can in some degree become sensitized organs of that Life. We are, nevertheless, our own very selves and we have autonomous sway over our own acts and wills. We are not swallowed up and lost in a One. In an august sense we control our own destiny and we build up the being that we are. The genuine spiritual universe seems to be a spiritual Society — a blessed community — which includes God and the cooperative souls, who with Him form the growing Kingdom of the spiritual Life.

He finds His complete Life in and through us as we find ours in and through Him and through each other in love and joy and cooperation. He needs us and we need Him, as a vine needs its branches and as the branches need the vine. The Spiritual Universe is thus a concrete reality, not an abstract one, and the Life of God can be revealed and has been actually revealed in a temporal life set in the midst of time, in the Christ of Galilee and Judea and in and through Christian History, in raised and transformed lives, lived through His power, and, as I have said, in the moral victories and demonstrations of the historical process.

This organic conception of the Life of God — a God in living, loving, saving operative relations with us — is already suggested in Saint Paul's Epistles and in Saint John's "Spirit of Truth" progressively revealing "all the Truth" through the generations of man. God in this interpretation is both immanent in the world — especially in the inner, deeper world of moral wills — and He is at the same time transcendent in the sense that He is forever more than any temporal expression or revelation of Himself. It belongs inherently to the very nature of Spirit — even finite spirit — to be self-transcendent, that is, to be more than any given utterance of itself. Enough has been said, I hope, to make it clear that I am here discovering and interpreting God as that central Reality in whom we live and move and are, and yet who respects our august privileges as persons. We can live in Him and for Him or we can go off on our own, insist on our freedom and waste our substance in egoistic ways of foolishness. We can read life down or read it up. We can see it as a temporal, empirical process, or we can assess it in its eternal significance. We can be centers of instinctive drives and urges, or we can be candles of the Lord, organs for the revelation of the Life of the Spirit. — Why 213–14

1

A Mutual and Reciprocal Correspondence

Rufus Jones was profoundly convinced that we dwell in a God-saturated cosmos in which all aspects of reality are woven together by the presence of Spirit. In our rush to categorize and classify the world, we frequently overlook this deep-down unity. We break the "uni-verse" into a "multi-verse" by contriving convenient dichotomies between subject and object, mind and body, spirit and matter. But these abstract distinctions run roughshod over our core intuition of a "mutual and reciprocal correspondence" between inner and outer landscapes. Without this inherent correspondence, which continuously recalls us to the truths that our spirit is kindred to God's and that all creation pulsates to the divine heartbeat, we would be exiled to a gray world barren of meaning or purpose.

In the selections that follow, Jones focuses on this correspondence from several different angles. He tells us that neither mind nor nature can be reduced to purely physical descriptions, and that we need a new psychology capable of taking soul and spirit seriously; suggests that the correspondence between God and humans is best understood as loving and open intimacy; argues *that the soul, because it carries a "divine spark," should never be thought of as depraved or fallen; and concludes by focusing on what the experiences of truth, beauty, and goodness can tell us about the deep nature of both the soul and the "More" with which it is indissolubly linked.*

THE OVER-WORLD

Emerson began his famous essay on *Nature* with the insistent claim that "the universe is composed of Nature and the Soul." Emerson meant by "Soul" what in these lectures I am calling "mind of the spirit type" — self-conscious organizing mind, the *nous* of the Greeks. We need to come back from thin behaviorist theories and scant pragmatist conceptions of mind and recover the mind's true amplitude and scope of creative activity. The moment the universe is sundered from organizing mind it can furnish no answers to any questions, nor can any questions be really asked about the things that matter to us. On that basis all accounts are closed. All slates are wiped clean. We are left indeed with a *tabula rasa*.

If our problems are ever to be solved, we must begin with a universe which includes mind — mind and Nature in mutual and reciprocal correspondence. It is not a spectator mind I am talking about here — a mind observing an outside show that goes on unaffected by the peephole observer. It is mind that has emerged out of the process of Nature and is kindred throughout with the world of deepest reality and is in give-and-take relations to it. I said in my first lecture: Nothing could have been more unexpected than the mutation which introduced a being with his face turned from the sod, and yet the environment was prepared to give this unpredictable emergent a welcome and a home when it arrived.

I also said in that earlier lecture that the spiritual, as we know it, is in some strange way superimposed on the physical, the biological, the natural; it is not a purely heavenly emergent; it comes as a new and subtle elevation of what was here before. There is undoubtedly close correlation between our conscious minds and the cortex of our brains, and to be accurate it would be necessary, of course, to extend the correlation far beyond the cortex, though that more inclusive physical substructure need not be dealt with in detail here.

But, unfortunately, we are confronted with the insuperable difficulty that nobody yet knows how brain and consciousness are related. Certain specific functions have been in a limited way located and mapped in the cortex, and the correlation is more exact and definite than was formerly supposed. But what we want most to know about we know least about — how to pass from vibrations or neural processes in the brain to consciousness in the mind. That is true of even the lower stages of consciousness. We do not know — nobody knows — how we get from sensory stimuli to consciousness of objects, from elemental *sensa* to concrete wholes of experience. It is so usual, so common, a happening, that we overlook the miracle of it. But it becomes an outstanding mystery when we rise to the level of free ideas, to our experience of duration-time, to the recovery of the past with the consciousness that it is *our* past, and with the anticipation of the future as our future, or to the appreciation of intrinsic values and the intimations of a Beyond to all our horizons of time and sense. Confronted with these higher stages of our life all theories so formed break down and we have as yet no convincing answers. The Copernicus, the Newton, has not appeared yet to bring a luminous trail of light into this region of darkness.

What we can say with some confidence is that the mind-world in which we live and have our being, our firsthand certainty — our *cogito ergo sum* assurance — is a miniature over-world of our own, not composed of cortex neurons or of vibrations, or of any physical substance. For centuries nobody knew that his over-world of consciousness had anything to do with a cortex in the brain. If persons of an earlier time linked it up at all with a physical substructure, it was with man's heart, or what he called his "reins," that is, his kidneys, or with his bowels (below his diaphragm). And our Bible talks of "bowels of mercy." As we know it and live *in* this inner world of ours, however we may explain its origin, it is a mind-world, above the brain, not of the brain class, or station, or level. The Archbishop of York [William Temple] said in his Gifford Lectures: "As mind increasingly takes control of the organism, so it becomes increasingly independent of the organism as physiologically conceived." The finished, completed brain, with its synapses and current paths, may be said at least to be as much produced by the mind-world as the mind-world is "caused" by the brain. In any case it is a cogent and striking example of an over-world of which we not merely have intimation but of which we *are* and to which we *belong*. If anything in the universe is real, this little over-world of our experience is real — this microcosmos of ours.

The only reason for calling it an "over-world" is the obvious fact that it is on a new level, above the physical, above the storm and whirl of molecular vibrations. Consciousness of our type is of an order all its own. No increase of our knowledge of what is taking place on the brain level would lead to an expectation of what occurs on this higher level. No microscopic observation of the neural system, even if it could be expanded a thousand times the present range of perceiving, would supply a basis for the prediction of the experiences of a conscious self above the wild neuronic cyclone. This mind realm is now — and, until the coming of the new Copernicus of the microcosmos, it will remain —

a mysterious over-world; but it is none the less *our own* world of undoubted reality, veracity, and validity. Everything else can be doubted except the reality of my thinking that I think and knowing that I know.

In the light of this little over-world of ours, above the world of molecular vibrations, it is a safe prediction, I think, that there is an Over-World of a higher order, above or within the entire macrocosmic system. There are, to say the least, many intimations of such an Over-World. I shall not of course be able to demonstrate this claim so that everybody will be bound to accept it as proved. These things by which we live do not admit of such inevitability or certainty as that. But minds of our type can have come from no lower Source than Mind of this higher Order, and the values which enrich our world of experience in times of high visibility at least bring with them implications of a Source that fits their unique status of reality. . . .

If we are to suggest an Over-World that is cogent today, it must have its ground and basis in the implications and intimations of our actual experience. It must tally with these minds of ours and with the whole of Nature with which we are organic. It must not be shot out of an air gun for the satisfaction of the shooter, or for the delight of the spectators. It is fairly obvious now, I think, that no adequate explanation of the things which matter most to us, the realities by which we live, is forthcoming by the method of exact description of observed phenomena, or by the method of explanation in terms of antecedent causation. Antecedent causation, if taken with rigor, involves an infinite regress, a "bad infinite" — a cause behind each cause, with no real cause ever in sight; and exact description, if taken seriously, involves ever-increasing analysis, with more and more minute residual elements, which at last offer no explanation of the extraordinary principles of concatenation and mathematical and logical order. Then, too, there are all the time mind-experiences, mind-realities, and mind-values, which do not submit to methods of description, or to causal explanation. You know them only by having them, and you can explain them only in terms of themselves.

So long as one stays on the level of elemental vibrations, or of any type of described external facts, one could never predict an Over-World of Mind. It is only when we begin to deal with the actual facts of mind-experience, with its given realities and implications, that we find the clue, the guiding thread, to ultimate and real explanations of what we have on our hands, and on our hearts. No discoveries about the nature of matter throw any light on the nature of mental activity, or upon the unique unity of the life of the mind. Professor [William Pepperell] Montague is right when he says that those who know least about matter think most of it, while those who know most of it think least of it, as an all-sufficient explanation. I am not a matter-despiser — matter is a friend rather than an enemy. It is an indispensable feature of this double world system to which we belong. My main contention is that the approach to our supremely important ultimates must be through the mind-path rather than through the matter-highway, though, if we are wise, we shall not pry them apart and deal with either sundered half of the total whole.

Let me now proceed to gather up the implications which point to what William James called "our Mother Sea" or, again in James' words, "the More" that is "coterminous and continuous" with our selves and operative in the universe, and which I prefer to call the "Over-World," revealed first of all as a Beyond within us.

We are already participating in this Over-World when we are immersed in the experience of the intrinsic values of Beauty, or of moral Goodness which ought to be, or of Truth which is eternally, inevitably true, or of Love for Love's sake. These are

all typical realities which come into view only when there is a
co-operating mind of what I have called the spirit-type. Only
an interpretative mind, endowed with imagination and supplied
with creative forms of judgment and appreciation, can create
and enjoy Beauty, or have the conviction of Ought, or experience the necessary character of Truth, or love with a Love that
suffers long, never lets go, is not provoked, endures and abides
when everything else is "done away."

Not only do these supreme realities involve a peculiar type of
mind on the subjective side; they equally involve a peculiar kind
of world on the objective side. The Nature that presents the
occasions for Beauty, Goodness, Truth, and Love is a Nature
no longer exactly describable and explainable as a congeries
of atoms and molecules and vibrations. It is a Nature deeply
interfused with Spirit — Coherence, Order, Concatenation, Law,
Logic, Mathematics, Significance, and Meaning. It is a sacramental universe through which Deep calleth unto Deep and
significant realities of the impalpable and intangible sort "break
in" on us and answer to our deepest being. We reach through
the veil of what we call matter and are in a higher World which
is kin to our minds and to which, as great amphibians, we really
belong. In fact we lie open-windowed to it and partake of it.
This Over-World of Beauty, Goodness, Truth, and Love is as
truly and obviously beyond the welter and storms of the processes of matter and the basic stuff of the universe as our minds
are above and beyond the swirl of the brain paths which somehow correlate with minds and appear to be the occasion for
thought.

A great many persons in the history of our race have found
themselves in direct communion with this Over-Soul of Spirit,
have felt resources of life flood into themselves, have been invaded with life from beyond the margins of themselves. Among
those who have had such experiences are some of the sanest,

some of the wisest and best-balanced, persons who have ever lived. They have been as sure of the reality of their experience of a divine Other as ever they were of the hills and fields and rivers of their native habitat.

It is obvious that a secondhand account of such an event makes a much paler impression on the hearer of it than does a firsthand experience of the event itself. We know only too well how often we have been bored by the description of remote scenes that some traveler labors to present to us by a wordy picture, and the more he elaborates the less we care for the faraway scenery and circumstances of his travel. Somewhat so, readers of mystical experiences are quickly surfeited and soon cry, "Hold, enough." But I have been studying the mystics of history and the contemporary ones all my life — studying them with microscopical care and critical insight — and I am convinced that, after the necessary reduction and elimination, there is a remarkable nuclear residue of reality left on our hands. The original mystical experience feels like a thrust from beyond. Something breaks in on the soul like the tides from the Ocean beyond the ocean where we bathe. Thoreau writes in his *Journal:* "With all your science, can you tell me how, and whence it is, that light comes into the soul?"

The great religions of the race, and peculiarly the religion of the Hebrew prophets and the religion which took its rise in the Headwaters of the vast Christian stream, are fundamentally grounded in experiences that came to great spiritual geniuses. They have been among the foremost builders of the structure of the human civilization. Most of our art and music and architecture and poetry has stemmed out of this source of life. I know the error and superstition and blunder and habit-drag that have gone along with this stream through the ages. But always at the source and always at the times of renewal and renascence there have been pillar personalities who have felt themselves in firsthand contact not with material realities, or with new economic facts, or with the discovery of larger food supplies, but with this Over-World of the Spirit. And thereby they have been able to heighten life at its inner source and to raise the level of life itself.

What we have on our hands, as we consider our universe, is not an endlessly rhythmic and homogeneous and repetitive system, every stage of which is predictable from the nature of the system itself. Our real universe, quite the contrary, is an evolving order, marked all the way up by unpredictable mutations, with unexpected emergents which inaugurated new epochs and changed the line of march of the entire process. And, on the whole, strangest of all, the process has been forward and upward. There have been "blackout" epochs, backslips and reversed eddies; but the moment one takes a long-sighted view, and a long-run estimate, there has plainly enough been an evolution and not a devolution. . . . There are good grounds for the prediction that the process is intelligible, is significant, and that the universe is going on, and is going somewhere, and means something.

So long as we are satisfied to confine our attention to exact description of what is, and to a study of antecedent causes, the dramatic features of the universe will necessarily escape us, and we shall get no intimation of an Intelligence operative throughout the unfolding drama. But when we approach the cosmic process and the history of man's life on the planet as a vast drama with its multiform scenes and acts, on the whole suggesting a significant *dénouement*, we shall once more see good grounds for concluding that there is an Over-World operating as an influencing feature of the entire world-drama. And it is just possible — to claim no more — that the intelligible goal of the whole mighty movement is working *a fronte* toward the unseen end, as ideals certainly do in our individual lives. We cannot consider the universe to be intelligible unless we can discover that it is significant, and it is not significant unless it is in some sense a spiritual drama....

We could not live, we could not even bear it without grinning, if we knew that the whole affair was an appalling Sisyphus episode of rolling a meaningless rock up hill, only to see it turn and roll down again to the stupid starting point — a dull repeatable operation with no meaning or purpose anywhere apparent. When the cosmic process does seem like that, and when life looks like a futile dance of ephemeral gnats, it is because we fail to deal with the *whole world* and are gazing at a little broken arc of it, as one might judge of the Parthenon by the badly broken torso of a single carving of Phidias. — SM 49–53, 55–62

SOUL-FORCE

Mahatma Gandhi has made our generation very familiar with the phrase "soul-force." His native word for it is *Satyagraha*, which is often loosely translated "non-violence." That negative phrase, however, only feebly expresses the positive significance of the original Indian word. Gandhi has steadily maintained that truth and love, exhibited undeviatingly in a life purified from fear, hate, injustice, and bitterness, are invincible forces of the soul, and that is essentially what he means by "soul-force." He said to me in 1926: "Faith in the conquering power of love and truth has gone all the way through my inmost being and nothing in the universe can ever take it from me."

... Gandhi bases his doctrine of soul-force upon the power of the human soul to be an organ of that one Reality behind all life. Mysticism is always bold, but Indian mysticism is peculiarly daring. It has held for more than two thousand years,

through its greatest exponents, that there is an interior depth
to the human soul which is in its essence uncreated and death-
less. It is beyond the changes of "is and was and will be." It is
absolutely real and inseparable from that eternal Reality that is
the Root and Basis of all that is. After exhausting every method
of expression and every ingenuity of thought to hint to human
ears the nature of this deepest reality behind the temporal and
fleeting things of the world, the Indian mystic is accustomed to
end his account of the unutterable with the words, "*That* art
thou." He identifies, in other words, the inmost being of his
own self with the inmost Reality in the universe. At one point
within what he calls himself, he believes that he enters, through
a mysterious gateway, the realm of all that is Real, and he dares
to say, "That am I." "That art thou."

His approach to reality is thus not through rocks and hills
and skies, not through molecular forces and the energies of
suns, not even through the sacred Himalayas, but through the
reality which reaches the highest degree of certainty to him, the
reality of his own mind. He begins, thus, not with books and
documents, not with traditions and external authorities, but
with the verity of conscious self-existence. The surest evidence
that the universe culminates in a type of reality which can be
called "spiritual" is to be found in the fact that when we pene-
trate the labyrinthine ways of our own mind we are already in
the realm of the spirit.

We need a new depth psychology of quite a different order
from that which the experts in abnormality have been giving us.
There is a large amount of reliable testimony, coming to us from
all peoples that have a literature, that persons, often of unusual
sanity and wisdom, have had invading contact in the depths of
their souls with the central creative Stream of Life, and have
thereby transcended the limitations of their species and have
become dynamic centers of spiritual energy. There is no more

reason for doubting the fact of such transformation than there is for doubting that iron plunged into the fire becomes itself transformed and penetrated with the fire, or that a needle of tempered steel may be magnetized until it becomes sensitive to the invisible magnetic currents which stream around it and can put itself into parallelism to them.

It seems only too obvious that the world which we see and touch is not an independent and self-sufficing substance. It carries in itself no explanation of itself. It is not Maya, an illusion or a shadow. It possesses some kind of reality. But there must be something more real and more truly self-explanatory beyond it, or in behind it, or interpenetrating it, if we could only get in to find it. But always that inferred Reality "in behind" remains "in behind," and eludes us as the other side of the moon does, the side which no one on earth has ever seen. We are forced by the usual way of approach to go from outside in and to infer the true nature of the inmost Real from our observation of outside reality, which is always typically material stuff. It is impossible to identify the most refined outward things with what is "in behind," since the one is obviously "material" and the other is assumed to be "spiritual," and we are always in danger of ending with the material, with which we began. We may perhaps find that we can succeed better in our pursuit of the spiritually real if we begin with what is indubitably spiritual to start with, the consciousness of our own self-existence and proceed from what we ourselves are.

The mystical doctrine of the union of the soul at its deepest center with the Soul of the universe is perhaps not explicitly present in Gandhi's idea of "soul-force," but he always implies that something vastly greater than man's will or thought or scheme or plan flows through the sincere and dedicated soul. The soul in its depth has the moral and spiritual universe behind it. The soul-center of a pure, sincere person becomes, in

Gandhi's view of life, a fountain of love and truth and wisdom, and when it keeps its selfish desires and its individual aims in complete abeyance so that the stream of life is pure, all the strength and love and truth of God flow through the soul of the person of that type. The soul becomes, in fact, a channel of the infinite Reality and an extraordinary center of energy. Emerson, as everybody knows, preached this doctrine of the soul as an organ of the Over-soul with serene eloquence, and was throughout his life, in the atmosphere of American practical realism, an untiring exponent of the exhaustless energy of man's soul in contact with the Over-soul.

This depth-view of the soul lies at the very heart of Johannine Christianity, though it is thought of there as an imparted gift of grace rather than as a native capacity: "He that shall drink of the water that I shall give him, it shall become in him a fountain of water springing up unto life eternal" (John 4:14). Here the eternal source of the Life as Spirit floods into the human spirit and flows out through the human channel. The parable of the Vine and its branches illustrates vividly in a familiar figure a vital union of the individual person at his interior depth with the Eternal Vine-stock, in which, as a mighty Ygdrasil Tree, the life-sap of the world has its home. And, once more, in exalted words we are told that "when the Spirit of Truth comes into operation in the lives of men He will lead men into all the Truth" (John 16:13).

This doctrine of soul-force to which some of the noblest of our race have borne witness, however, flies pretty straight in the face of present day psychological theories of the soul. The "soul" has been passing through a time of depression, and seems to many persons down and out. It takes courage even to be on friendly terms with this poor outcast. Most writers have stopped speaking of the soul, and some timid preachers pause in their sermons to apologize for still using the "bedraggled word."

But we need not be too much overawed in what concerns the deepest issues of life by the conclusions of modern psychology. Psychology is not yet at a stage in its development when it can speak with authority or lay down infallible laws for the control of our spirits. It is bound to miss, as all scientific approaches do miss, the inmost reality of things. The psychological approach to the problem of the soul and to all other problems of life is in terms of description, and it still remains on the outside. It treats the mind as a series of events. Its basis of operation is that of an outside spectator. Its method is observation. It accumulates and interprets facts and processes of experience, not experience as it is felt. Genuine psychology, after the manner of science in general, is modest in its claims and presuppositions. It prescribes restraint. It endeavors to keep within its limited field of description and observation of observed facts.

As soon as psychology goes beyond the sphere of description of mental phenomena and enters upon that of explanation, it usually inclines to a theory of brain causation to account for mental facts. It also adopts the view that sensations are due to the impact of the external world upon the receptive organs of sense. Both of these theories obviously transcend observation. They both pass from actual experience to a metaphysical interpretation of it. It is no doubt the most obvious and natural form of explanation, but it is none the less metaphysical interpretation, not observation. Psychologists have taken this direction because it seemed to them to be the simplest one to take and because it was thought to involve a minimum of metaphysical theory.

But whether this method of explanation involves a minimum of metaphysics or not, it does, nevertheless, rest in the last analysis on metaphysical interpretation, not on observation. It is interpretation, not direct empirical approach. It transcends experience and it introduces something that has not been observed and something which from the nature of the case never can be observed. Furthermore, it has the disadvantage of laboring to explain a spiritual fact, a state of consciousness, a directly felt experience, by something wholly unlike it. There is nowhere else in the universe a parallel to the chasm between *a fact of conscious experience in the mind* and *molecular currents in the physical substance of the brain* that are assumed to be the "cause" of the conscious experience. Nor is there any possible way in sight of explaining how "impacts" of physical things in an external world could possibly produce consciousness of objects or, for that matter, any kind of mental states in a realm which is not physical.

No bridge over either of these chasms is yet known to us. We cross both chasms by a leap, and we leave the method of the leap unexplored. We go on talking as though molecular currents "produced" thought and as though outside impacts "caused" mental states, although our ignorance here is as deep as night. Some day a new Copernicus in the field of psychology will clarify the issue, and he will almost certainly clarify it by discovering that what we have been calling "physical" or "material" or "molecular" is vastly more interpenetrated by "spirit" than we have usually supposed. There is undoubtedly a remarkable fit between the inward and the outward. It is like the fit of the glove to the hand or like the two blades to a pair of scissors. The outward and the inward are certainly not divided by an absolute chasm. The object of our knowledge is not an absolute other to the mind that experiences it. They belong together as truly as do the convex and concave sides of a curve, and no man can put them asunder. If we begin with a spiritual center at the heart of our process of knowledge, we must be ready to go on and admit that there is a corresponding spiritual core within the universe itself.   — TS 163, 164–71

DIVINE SPIRIT
AND HUMAN SPIRITS

It was one of the difficult, in fact, insoluble, problems of ancient philosophy to find out what supported, or held up the world. It was easy to suppose that it rested on the back of some giant creature, but then came the chilling question, What holds up your giant creature? Each answer always led to another question. The answer at last is: It rests on nothing outside itself. There is no granite foundation underneath, nor is there any giant creature. Its substance is of such a nature that it feels a mighty attraction for every particle of matter in the visible universe. The sun, being the greatest body in our system, exerts upon it the strongest attraction, and this invisible, intangible power or force holds it like a woven cable and swings it safely in its ellipse. We say, then, that it belongs to the nature of matter to feel an affinity for other matter, however remotely the particles may be separated, and were this not so, no means could ever be found for holding up a world in space.

There is another question which has been almost equally difficult of solution: What is the explanation, the ground, the basis of religion? On what authority shall we build our faith? How do we know that there is any more reality back of our faith than there is back of our dreams? Then we have the common answers: God has given us a book which is an ultimate authority, and which declares the reality of things not seen. Or again: God has founded a church in this world by supernatural means. The founders of that church were divinely ordained and their decisions were infallibly right. They have transferred their authority to their successors and we have now in church traditions and church officials an authority which is a sure ground for faith, and which establishes the desired reality.

Either of these answers will do, until someone unkindly raises

the question which is sure to come sooner or later: How do
we know that the Bible is God's book to us, and, if so, who
is infallibly authorized to tell us what it means, in every line
of it? And secondly, what proof have we that the founders of
the church were divinely ordained and possessed of infallible
authority, and, if so, on what ground do we assert that their
successors, or the church traditions, have such divine sanction
as to make them authoritative? It is the old difficulty of finding
a support for our first support — what does your giant creature
stand on while he holds up the earth?

It may be well to postpone our search for an external authoritative basis of religion, until we have first looked to see whether
there be anything within man himself, and in his relationships,
which accounts for religion. If we start with a nature totally foreign to God, an insulated personality, windowless for light from
Him, and incapable of recognizing such light if it did come — then
it is hard to see how man could ever have any immediate certainty
of a divine reality, or where we could find a reasonable basis for
religion. If God could not and did not have a witness to Himself
within our human spirits it is difficult to see how we could ever
expect to establish the reality of His being, or have any sustained
assurance of His love. We gave up the problem of squaring the
circle because we now know enough about the problem to know
that it cannot be solved. It may as confidently be asserted that
a God who is not self-revealing, who has no relationship with
human spirits, who does not have a witness in human consciousness, could never be found, and the search for a basis of religion
on those conditions would of necessity have to be given up. The
entire agnosticism of our time grows out of the fact that thoughtful men have discovered the hopelessness of finding God either
in or back of the phenomena of nature. It is now clear that no
increase of either microscope or telescope will ever show Him.
Push back as far as ever we may, we find only forces, no God.

They are all looking for Him where He could not possibly be found. In a different path lies our true search for the "Holy Grail." The essential fact of religion is love, and love is impossible apart from relationships. Until two spirits can meet, and, in some degree, understand and appreciate each other, there can be no love. It begins with spiritual interrelation. The cloud and the clod are mere describable phenomena; they can be reduced to exact description. *Love* is forever *in*describable. It is felt and appreciated, or it remains unknown. The moment, therefore, we get beyond the traditional God, who is external and one "thing" among many things, as was the case, for instance, among the Greeks, we must not expect to find Him apart from spiritual relationships. It is in our consciousness of His love, in our appeal from our limited self to His infinite self, in that unmistakable, though indescribable, sense that we are interrelated parts of one Self who loves us, and who enfolds us, that a religion of any worth becomes possible. We know, when we love a human soul, that we can transcend our bodily isolation, our physical insularity, and that our spirit can share its life with another spirit. But no description of love could ever account for this, or be the basis of it, for souls who could not themselves so share and appreciate each other. So, too, there could be no religion of this higher sort, and the agnostics would be right, were it not for the fact — the supreme fact — that the divine Spirit and the human spirit come together and have spiritual relations together and witness to each other. Our religion — any religion on a high level — begins with the fact that it belongs to the essential life of God to impart Himself, to give Himself in love, in sympathy and in fellowship, and to share His life with men; and with the secondary fact that we are capable of appreciating such love when we see it and of responding to it.

We start out, then, boldly, with this primary fact that there is no necessary dualism between men and God — between the divine Spirit and human spirits. Their natures are not foreign and unrelated. There is but one possible separation between them, namely, sin, which, like a cataract destroys vision, not the light, and which, once removed, leaves the two spirits face to face. God and the human spirit belong together, in as real a sense as the light and the eye do, or beauty and the artist's soul, or harmony and the musician's ear. Who ever felt the necessity of proof that the sun was shining? In fact it makes itself known through closed lids. What greater proof could there be than that we see it? How could you ever prove to a tone-deaf man that Beethoven's symphonies are beautiful, or to a color-blind man that a sunset sky is glorious? There is no convincing authority; there can be no convincing authority beyond this appeal to consciousness. This appeal to consciousness carries conviction and wins assent because the human spirit has a capacity for truth, because it is not wholly foreign in nature to Him who is the truth. As we come into this world so furnished in the structure of our mind that we must view all objects in space and all events in time, so also we come with souls capable of recognizing truth and of responding to love and of assenting to righteousness when they present themselves; otherwise we never could learn to prize such things. It is with this in mind that Pascal explains religion in the famous words: "Thou wouldst not seek me if thou hadst not already found me."

The basis of religion, on the human side, is to be sought therefore in the nature of the human spirit itself; in its ability to respond to God because of a kinship to Him; in its capacity for truth and righteousness and its power of recognizing them as such; in the possibility of heart-purity, so that God may be spiritually perceived and known, and finally, in that act of choice and cooperation by which the human soul becomes transformed into a divine likeness and may attain to a union of self with the Father of Spirits. These facts — and without them there is no explanation of religion — will enable us now to find a basis for faith, for revelation, for church authority, for the communion and fellowship of saints and for the ground that religion is an endless characteristic of man — as sure to abide as consciousness is.   — DF 1–7

A SOUL HAS NO WALLS

As worship, taken in its highest sense and widest scope, is man's loftiest undertaking, we cannot too often return to the perennial questions: What is worship? Why do we worship? How do we best perform this supreme human function? Worship is too great an experience to be defined in any sharp or rigid or exclusive fashion. The history of religion through the ages reveals the fact that there have been multitudinous ways of worshiping God, all of them yielding real returns of life and joy and power to large groups of men. At its best and truest, however, worship seems to me to be *direct, vital, joyous, personal experience and practice of the presence of God.*

The very fact that such a mighty experience as this is possible means that there is some inner meeting place between the soul and God; in other words, that the Divine and human, God and man, are not wholly sundered. In an earlier time, God was conceived as remote and transcendent. He dwelt in the citadel of the sky, was worshiped with ascending incense and communicated His will to beings beneath through celestial messengers or by mysterious oracles. We have now more ground than ever before for conceiving God as transcendent; that is, as above and beyond any revelation of Himself, and as more than any finite experience can apprehend. But at the same time, our experience and our ever-growing knowledge of the outer and inner universe confirm our faith that God is also immanent, a real presence, a spiritual reality, immediately to be felt and known, a vital, life-giving environment of the soul. He is a Being who can pour His life and energy into human souls, even as the sun can flood the world with light and resident forces, or as the sea can send its refreshing tides into all the bays and inlets of the coast, or as the atmosphere can pour its life-giving supplies into the fountains of the blood in the meeting place of the lungs; or, better still, as the mother fuses her spirit into the spirit of her responsive child, and lays her mind on him until he believes in her belief.

It will be impossible for some of us ever to lose our faith in, our certainty of, this vital presence which overarches our inner lives as surely as the sky does our outer lives. The more we know of the great unveiling of God in Christ, the more we see that He is a Being who can be thus revealed in a personal life that is parallel in will with Him and perfectly responsive in heart and mind to the spiritual presence. We can use as our own the inscription on the wall of the ancient temple in Egypt. On one of the walls a priest of the old religion had written for his divinity: "I am He who was and is and ever shall be, and my veil hath no man lifted." On the opposite wall, someone who had found his way into the later, richer faith, wrote this inscription: "Veil after veil have we lifted and ever the Face is more wonderful!"

It must be held, I think, as Emerson so well puts it, that there is "no bar or wall in the soul" separating God and man. We lie open on one side of our nature to God, who is the Oversoul of our souls, the Overmind of our minds, the Overperson of our personal selves. There are deeps in our consciousness which no private plumb line of our own can sound; there are heights in our moral conscience which no ladder of our human intelligence can scale; there are spiritual hungers, longings, yearnings, passions, which find no explanation in terms of our physical inheritance or of our outside world. We touch upon the coasts of a deeper universe, not yet explored or mapped, but no less real and certain than this one in which our mortal senses are at home. We cannot explain our normal selves or account for the best things we know — or even for our condemnation of our poorer, lower self — without an appeal to and acknowledgment of a Divine Guest and Companion who is the real presence of our central being.   — IL 97–101

INNER LIGHT

When the "heretics" of the different periods proclaimed their new Pentecosts and called attention to the inrushing energies of the Spirit, they were apt to find their evidence in abnormal phenomena and in rare and mysterious occurrences. They did not yet realize that the surer and sounder evidence of the Spirit is to be found in normal, everyday processes of life, that "the everlasting sign" is that slow transformation of our stubborn nature, so that the balsam comes in and the thorns go out; the sweet myrtle appears where the briers used to be.

We know light as luminosity or pure radiance and we know light as it is revealed in the color band of the spectrum. But that does not exhaust it. There is still a third manifestation of light as wonderful as the other two. This third aspect of light is its radiant energy, its photochemical, or actinic energy, as it is usually called. It works remarkable effects upon sensitive plates. It is, too, a vital energy, operating upon and energizing all life, producing that vital substance we call chlorophyll in plants and vitamins in food. Light as energy is a resident power. It is present where it operates. The sun is not only a material body ninety-six million miles away, it is also just as truly *here*, in the vital, actinic effects which our vast and various orders of life reveal. No light, no life. So, too, we must go on to speak of God as resident, immanent, *God with us*, a vital, revealing, energizing presence, using man as the organ of His unending operation and revelation in the world.

If this is true, it is a very important fact about man — the most important fact about him — and it means that we must think of man henceforth in different terms from those that have prevailed in the great theological systems of the past. It involves a Copernican revolution as profound and far-reaching as that which has reorganized all our astronomical thinking. Man can hardly be considered as a poor worm in the dust, if he has a capacity for God and can become an organ of divine revelation. We cannot accept at their face value statements which affirm the moral depravity of man, if God and man, as we must believe, are essentially related. This low estimate of man and these pessimistic theories of man's nature are partly responsible for the long centuries of the perversion of Christianity, for the calm acceptance of war as a normal part of life and for the base treatment of man by man.

This medieval account of man, as morally depraved, it should be said, rests upon a great epic view of the universe which has gradually given place to a truer view, based upon verified facts. The classical account of this epic view of the universe — one of the greatest epics in human history — was written by St. Augustine of Hippo in his *City of God,* and it was accepted for the next fourteen centuries as though it were absolute and final truth....

It was a work of extraordinary genius, as much as is Chartres Cathedral or the greatest pictures of the Madonna....It seemed to rest upon unquestioned authority and it gave an immense ground and support for the growing imperial conception of the Church. Man was unable to do anything toward his own salvation. He stood before God without the least claim of merit. He was utterly dependent upon the Church, which was the one and only vehicle of Grace, the mysterious instrument of salvation in a wrecked world. When once this theory of man had become established as an essential part of the faith of Christendom and was woven into the very fiber of Christian consciousness, it enjoyed long immunity from criticism and was accepted without serious examination, in the same way as the theory of the four elements of matter survived century after century.

Wherever deep and solitary souls in the Middle Ages turned away from ecclesiasticism and dogma to try the venturesome paths of firsthand experience, this ancient construction of theology dropped out of focus, and these persons, the great mystics, speaking with the authority of inner conviction, asserted that there was something in the very structure of man which linked him to God. Their interpretation of man's inner being was often put into cumbersome scholastic phraseology, which was the best they could do, but at any rate the fact got affirmed that there was a divine spark at the apex of the soul, or as others put it, a divine soul center or ground, which kept man, here in the midst of time and mutability, unsundered from the great spiritual Reality who was his origin and home....

The Quakers in the seventeenth century gave this message a new and powerful emphasis. In fact, they form the first organized body of Christians who built their entire faith upon the principle that something of God is present in every man. They broke completely with the Augustinian conception of man, raised in their time to a new stage of importance by John Calvin's impressive interpretation of it. Their famous phrase was the "inward Light," or the "Divine Seed," which they set over against the Calvinistic view of man, who was thought of as totally corrupt and beginning life handicapped by the inheritance of seeds of sin implanted in the soul. Quakerism, in its historical significance, can be rightly understood

only as a profound revolt against the Calvinistic interpretation
of man.

The Quakers meant by their inward Light what the noblest
of the mystics had meant by the divine ground or foundation of
the soul. They believed that man is not separated by a chasm or
isolated from God. Something of God, something of that highest spiritual Nature — that World within the world we see —
is formed into the structure of the human soul, so that it is
never, even though "born and banished into mystery," beyond
hail of its true source and home, and never without the possibility of divine assistance and communion. The early Quakers,
like their mystical predecessors, were weak in psychology and
were unable to think out the full import of their experience
or of their significant phrase, the "inward Light," but in any
case they broke with that ancient epic theory of man which
their contemporary, John Milton, just at that very time was doing so much to glorify. They leaped to the position that each
newborn child is a new Adam fresh from the creative hand of
God and bears within him the mark of a divine origin and of
a divine destiny. He comes to his great experiment here in this
strange mixed world equipped with something which only God
Himself could have put in him, something spiritual, something
capable of vital response to the environing presence of the living Spirit. He may live upward or he may live downward, for
he is free to choose, but he can never wholly obliterate the spiritual endowment which makes him something more than "mere
man." In the hush and silence of the corporate group which the
Quakers raised to an immense importance, they believed man
could become aware of that More than himself revealed within
himself.

Not only has man something spiritual in the foundation of
his being, but the Quakers further believe that God is essentially Spirit. He is Life and Thought and Love and Goodness

in unceasing revelation and action. He is the near and constant environment of the soul, as surely as the ocean is the environment of the islands which rise out of it. The reason there could once be a supreme revelation of God in one historical Person was just because God can pour His Spirit around and through a sensitive, receptive Life that wills to be an organ of His manifestation. The religious life for a man truly begins with the personal discovery of these inner divine resources. Man leaps into life and power as soon as he begins to recognize and appreciate the springs of spiritual energy ready at his hand to be drawn upon by his own initiative of will. From beginning to end religion is vital — it is cooperation and fellowship with God. It is drawing in and sending forth the vital energies of the resident Spirit.

The faith of the Quaker in the inward Light does not rest upon traditional authority, it is not a theory constructed out of ancient texts. It is, in so far as it is vital and significant, a fact of experience. Inward Light, if it is to be real, something more than a phrase, must be something *seen* and *felt* and *known*. Light is light only when it is apprehended and responded to by an awakened consciousness aware of it. Inward Light ceases to be of any value to the world as soon as it is turned into a dull, scholastic theory, hidden away in a leather-covered book. The whole significance of the Quaker movement was its revolt from theories and notions and its appeal instead to experience. There has always been, however, a subtle tendency to slide back to the sovereignty of phrases and to suppose that spiritual battles could be won by coining a magic word. But if we have no testimony of consciousness to God's immediate presence, if we cannot say, as George Fox could: "I know God experimentally and have the key that opens," it is in vain for us to talk of *theories* of inward Light.

If this great experience is real, as it appears to be, and if the claim which the Quakers have made for two centuries and a half is sound, namely, that *God reveals Himself in man*, then they have discovered a new fact about man, something which the Augustinian theology did not sufficiently know. According to this view, a Beyond always reveals itself within. Man is always and everywhere himself plus a More than himself. He is a finite center through which an infinite and eternal Spirit works and acts. To be man is to be more than the fragment called "mere man," just as we now know that matter is never "mere matter"; it consists of centers of tension where transcending energies break through and reveal themselves. There is no such thing as *matter by itself*.

Wherever there is matter there is an exhibition of cohesion, gravitation, and other forces which sweep beyond and transcend the tiny fragment called "matter." The entire universe is behind the fragment....

God is Spirit and therefore reveals Himself at the highest and best through man who, in his measure, is also spirit. Some men live downward and focus their attention upon things that are seen and tangible. They hardly believe any testimony of man's spiritual nature. There are others, however, who live out beyond the fringes of the things they see and handle and are all the time aware of intimation clear of wider scope. They care little for formal arguments to prove God's existence, for they no longer seek for a God on Olympus or above the sky or outside somewhere, working as an architect. God for them is the rational foundational ground of all that is real. We find Him when we enjoy beauty. We prove Him whenever we discover truth. We are with Him and in Him whenever we love with a love which rises above self and gives itself to another. He is there whenever we suffer and agonize over sin and wrong, and dedicate our will to make righteousness and goodness triumph.

So we do not need to go "somewhere" to find God. We only

need to *be* something. We need to hate our sin and failure, our pettiness and narrowness of vision, to come back home from the arid land of the stranger, and to rise from our isolated, solitary aims and be merged in life and spirit with Him who is knocking at our souls, and lo! we have found Him and He is ours and we are His.   —RF 30–33, 34–36, 40–41

THE BEYOND WITHIN

Is there any reality within our sphere which transcends time and space, and which thus may be a gateway of approach to a World of supersensuous reality such as we demand for genuine religion? Yes, there is. The knowing self within us by whatever name it is called — mind, soul, self-as-knower, I myself, or central personality — belongs to a different order from that of observed phenomena. Plato made the point very clear in his day, and his greatest disciples have enlarged upon it, that the mind, the soul, which he called the *nous* in us, which organizes the facts of experience, the data of experience, and interprets them by means of universal and particular forms of thought, cannot itself at the same time be *one of the facts to be experienced.* The *nous* in us must have had its origin in, and must belong to, a higher World order, the World of *Nous* — Spirit....

One of our most common blunders is that of treating the mind as though it were only a spectator. There is, however, in beings of our type no real mind that is merely a spectator-mind, that merely "receives" and "observes" presented facts. Every mind which deserves that name unifies, organizes, and interprets everything that is presented to it. There is, therefore, something presupposed in the nature of mind which did not come from outside nor arise out of change and process. Change and process are facts *for it*, not the ground of its being....

There is, furthermore, a unity to the knowing mind, which no observed facts in the outside world can fully account for. There is nothing like it in the world of relativity, and there is nothing outside itself which can explain it. The kind of mind which is essential for what we mean by knowledge, by truth, the mind which imposes its universal and necessary forms upon all that it knows, has no counterpart anywhere in the world of process and relativity. It is a unique reality. It belongs to a different order.

This unique mind goes beyond everything which sense reports as given fact, and anticipates by imaginative forecast what is to be, but not yet. The mind may by a flash of insight, by a stroke of genius, announce a law of nature which in its operation reaches far beyond all observed facts and which determines in advance of further perception whole vast areas of facts and events in regions not yet explored. Something similar is true in the realm of ideal goodness and, again, in the realm of creative art. Ethical insight may enable a person to anticipate a form and type of goodness that never has actually been before, but now is made real in this actual world, through this man's creative ideal. So, too, the synoptic mind of an artist may produce a beautiful creation which transcends in unity and harmony any object that has previously existed in the world of things....

What I am leading up to is the point that minds of this type — and we all possess some of this organizing and creative capacity — go beyond what is, surmise the more yet, transcend the given, have the inward power to see the invisible and to live in correspondence with a Beyond which is absolutely real. Beings of that scope and range are something more than "forked radishes with heads fantastically carved," or "unfeathered bipeds with broad flat tails." They partake of another order, another level of reality to that of the biological series. They are spiritual beings. They belong in a noumenal order and have correspondence with an Over-world, in spite of the fact that they have visible bodies with avoirdupois weight, that they consume food, and often do foolish things.

Not only do these minds of ours expand life in ideal directions and go beyond what is, but at their best these ideals of ours correlate and correspond with some sort of objective reality. They advance truth. They set forward the march of goodness. Through cooperation with God they build a new stage of the Kingdom of God in the world. We are in that respect not dreamers; we are actual builders. We exercise a dominion over events. We carry the ball on toward the goal. Something not ourselves co-works with us, as the currents of the ocean co-work with the mariner who is traveling in their direction. Something more than our finite will pushes behind our effort. Something large and luminous backs our deeds. When we are on right lines of advance, doors open before us. We find ourselves in cooperative union with a larger Mind and a wiser Will. We have sound reason to believe that what is highest in us is deepest in the nature of things. We become organs of a spiritual kingdom and stand in vital relation to an Eternal Mind and Heart and Will with whom we cooperate.

There is something in us and of us that did not originate in the world of matter, in the time-space order, in the phenomenal process. We are more than curious bits of the earth's crust, more than biological exhibits. We have a spiritual lineage. We may have collateral connections with flat-nosed baboons, but at the same time we are of direct noumenal origin. We belong to an Over-world of a higher order. We carry in the form and structure of our inner selves the mark and badge of linkage and kinship with a realm which can best be called Eternal, since it is real in its own essential being and of the same nature as God who is the center of its life and of ours.

Men in all ages, ever since there were men, have felt this

Beyond within themselves. They have traveled out beyond the frontiers of the seen, and have lived in mutual correspondence with the More that is akin to themselves. Saints and prophets and supreme revealers of the race have interpreted for the others vividly and vitally the splendor of their unique insights and contacts. But first, last, and all the time, religion has lived and flourished because man in his inner deeps is in mutual and reciprocal correspondence with eternal reality, and is in some measure the organ of it. We are religious beings because we partake or may partake of this higher Nature and share by our inmost form of being in a realm that is eternally real. At one apex point within ourselves we break through the world of change and process and belong to another order which may become our fatherland and home. Religion at its best is the discovery of home and fatherland.　　—TS 63–70

2

Living and Active
Mysticism

As we saw in the last chapter, the correspondence between inner and outer landscapes means that the soul is innately open to God's presence. Everyone is capable of a deep-seated and grounding experience of the Divine — or, as Jones says, everyone is potentially a mystic. We're all born with the capacity to savor the world as God's resplendent medium, but our spiritual sensibilities dull when we leave the innocence of childhood. To recapture our original talent for seeing creation as the God-infused wonder it is, we must cultivate "new eyes," the "eyes of an enlightened heart." We must experience the "vital surge of fresh life" that comes from genuine mysticism.

The following selections represent the heart of Jones's teaching on the mystical way. In them he tells us that mysticism is a lived and active experience that stills the longing of our hearts by bringing us into ever closer fellowship with God. But this does not mean turning one's back on the world and striving in solitude for intensely ecstatic moments in which we lose all sense of self. On the contrary, a genuine mystical relationship with God is built squarely within the world. Our best chance of discov-

ering God is by searching for the Infinite in the finite, and our best chance of truly communing with God is when the self is at its best, not when the self has been negated. Then mystical experience becomes a habitual way of being in which we joyfully serve as God's co-workers. Mysticism, in short, is not a spiritual gift for the privileged few, but the natural consequence of our inherent openness to God.

EVERYONE A MYSTIC

I am convinced by my own life and by wide observation of children that mystical experience is much more common than is usually supposed. Children are not so absorbed as we are with things and with problems. They are not so completely organized for dealing with the outside world as we older persons are. They do not live by cut-and-dried theories. They have more room for surprise and wonder. They are more sensitive to intimations, flashes, openings. The invisible impinges on their souls and they feel its reality as something quite natural.

Wordsworth was no doubt a rare and unusual child, but many a boy, who was never to be a poet, has felt as he did. "I was often unable," he says, in the preface to his great "Ode," "to think of external things as having external existence, and I communed with all that I saw as something not apart from, but inherent in, my own immaterial nature. Many times while going to school have I grasped at the wall or tree to recall myself from this abyss of idealism to the reality."

The world within is just as real as the world without until events force us to become mainly occupied with the outside one.

—FT 10–11

NEW EYES

We must somehow recover our power to see essential realities vividly. It demands new eyes — what the Bible calls *vision*. Our optical structure, with its marvelous retinal system of rods and cones, and its adjustable lens, is well fitted for the perception of colors and shapes of objects, for dealing with the visible choir of heaven and the furniture of earth. We have immensely enlarged its scope, both upward and downward, by the invention of telescopes and microscopes. These inventions have enabled us to discover objects that were never dreamed of in ancient astronomy and physics. Here were "new eyes" that could see in heaven and on earth objects which old unaided eyes were forever bound to miss. Nobody knew that the planet Jupiter had moons until Galileo's telescope found them. Nobody suspected the inside mysteries of plant and flower until the microscope made them common properties, which are familiar to school boys and school girls now.

But there are realities of a different order which no increase of the microscope or telescope will ever reveal, which rods and cones and lenses are not made to deal with. "We look," St. Paul said, "not at things that are seen with the eyes, but at things that are not seen, for seeable things are temporal but things which eyes cannot see are eternal." It is for *that* that "new eyes" are needed.

This great passage of St. Paul is of course an instance of oriental over-emphasis. He is so impressed with the importance of seeing invisible realities that he tells us not to look at the things that are seen. But we should probably never find the invisibles if we wholly neglected the visible world. We are more apt to find the invisible Reals by looking *through* the visibles, as the medium. We should never have discovered the laws of the universe if we had neglected to observe the objects through which the laws are revealed. What St. Paul would say if he were here now would be something like this: "You belong to two worlds; do not miss the invisible one while you are busy with the visible one. Cultivate your *vision*, learn to see the realities which your eyes miss. Look through the world that is seen and discover the realities which it suggests and implies."

This other kind of perception, with the "new eyes," turns out to be an essential feature of life. It is not a luxury; it is a necessity. "Where *vision* fails the people perish." Again and again the experts in the domain of life tell us that it is persons who endure as seeing the invisibles that build the permanent civilizations of the world.

The "eyes" I am talking about, the eyes that see the invisibles, do not belong to a chosen few persons, the spiritually elite; they belong, potentially at least, to all of us who have minds. When Wordsworth said that "Imagination is Reason in its most exalted mood," he was using "imagination" as the capacity to *see* the realities by which we live. We all do it in our measure, but it is a capacity which can be cultivated, improved, expanded, as certainly as the capacity to see perspective is cultivated by the artist. Most of us see objects with innocence of eye, without any attention to perspective, while the artist sees everything as he would draw it.

Open the Bible almost anywhere at random and you will find a sentence beginning with the word "Behold." It is calling upon the reader to use all his powers to *see* what rods and cones are bound to miss. We are being asked to see with "new eyes." This call to "behold" expresses surprise, wonder, thrill, joy, admiration. It is an attitude which we express with the exclamation point. If we could learn how to *behold* with new eyes we could more often supplement the interrogation point with the exclamation point of wonder and awe.

We have been living for several generations now in the era

of the interrogation point. We have written the question mark all over the earth and the sky, probing endlessly for causes and origins, pushing back the skirts of time and the canopies of space with our never-ceasing questions, What? Whence? Why? We have written this question mark over every holy book and every sacred place. We have invaded the inner deeps of the soul with our crooked, crabbed question mark and we have asked that interior dweller of ours to stand and deliver its mysteries.

We all recognize, of course, that the use of the question mark is one way to truth. We cannot dispense with it and we must not rail against it and call it, as Lowell did, "the devil's crook Episcopal." But the time has come, I am sure, to return to the way of wonder and to *see* with the eyes of joy and admiration, the eyes that see the invisibles. We should find our way more frequently to the discovery of God, if we cultivated more effectively our power to *see*, with reason in its most exalted mood, and learned how to make the response of joy and wonder. Nowhere else in literature is this type of creative vision at such a noble level as in the Bible, and nowhere is this feeling of surprise and wonder raised to such a lofty stage....

To see the eternal in the midst of time, to feel and to enjoy the infinite here in the finite, is one of the greatest blessings life has to offer. Plato used to say that life comes to its full glory when some beautiful object, or some loved person, suddenly opens for us a window that gives a glimpse into eternal reality. It is no doubt a satisfaction to know causes and to understand and explain what before was mysterious, but even greater is the thrill when something breaks in on our souls that is exactly as it ought to be, which is what occurs with consummate beauty. It is a state beyond mere knowledge. We now both know and adore, because we *see*....

But how are we ever in this busy and material world going

to realize all this? We must have new eyes — the eyes of our heart enlightened. That means that we must see essential realities vividly. We must have our imagination captured. Matthew Arnold said that conduct is three-fourths of life. But it isn't. Getting your imagination captured is almost the whole of life. The minute the eyes of your heart are enlightened, the minute your imagination gives you the picture of your path, your goal, your aim — it is as good as done. The way to become the architect of your fate, the captain of your soul, is to have your imagination captured.

We talk about the momentous will, but you tug at your will in vain until imagination dominates the scene, and at once you are on the way to your goal. There is no other way to spiritual victory except by having the eyes of the heart enlightened. That is the way you saddle and bridle and control your instincts and emotions. This happens to be the psychology not only of St. Paul and St. Augustine but of William James as well. "Consent to an idea's undivided presence at the focus of attention," our Harvard psychologist declares, "and action follows immediately." That is what I meant by the capture of the imagination — the guiding idea for the will.

But we all know that there is something deeper than thinking or willing, a subsoil, an abysmal inner life, out of which ideas and ideals emerge like capes of cloud out of the invisible air. The master secret of life is to feed or to fertilize that inner depth-life by worship, by meditation, by great literature of reality. Thus the eyes of the heart are enlightened. Thus one may out of the shadow see:

> *The high-heaven dawn of more than mortal day*
> *Strike on the Mount of Vision.*
>
> —NE 1–7, 12–14

AT-HOMENESS

The essential characteristic of the mystical experience is the attainment of personal conviction by an individual that the human spirit and the divine Spirit have met, have found each other, and are in mutual and reciprocal correspondence as spirit with Spirit. In short, mystical devotion means direct first-hand fellowship with God, and the deepened life-results which emerge.

We all begin life by simply living, not by following a program or a theory or a system. The roots of life are too deep for diagnosis. They escape our analysis. We follow the push of a life-impulse. There is a vital urge which carries us forward. The little lips of the baby feel the mother's breast and the right action follows. Correspondence with environment is life's main miracle. There is a fit of inner and outer, like that of hand and glove. But from the first the approach is deep, hidden, uncogitated, mystical. The outer world presents its stimulus, sometimes as gentle as the vibrations of light, or the touch of a soft finger, and the response comes from within with infallible skill and with an untaught wisdom which may as well as not be called a "mystical" correspondence. So, too, with the birth of religion. There is here once more a within and a without, a tiny finite being and a Beyond, a spiritual center and a vaster environment, and they feel and find one another as the retina does light, or as the electrode finds its polar mate. It begins, as life does, not with a scheme or a theory, but with living and being and responding. In short, both life and religion are rooted in mystical experience, mystical process.

There are, of course, all degrees of intensity and of attainment, as is true of any supreme human undertaking. As this purpose to find God for one's life aim is man's highest undertaking, it would naturally be expected to run through a wide gamut. It may begin, as in St. Augustine's case, with the discovery that our hearts are restless and that only one Reality in the universe will still that restlessness. It may appear as an exalted aspiration for personal contact with God as in the cry of the Psalmist: "As the hart panteth after the water brooks, so panteth my soul after Thee, O God. My soul thirsteth for God, for the living God." It may be the victorious flight of the soul from all earthly nests of ease and from all its secular perchings on things that perish to find the One Eternal Reality for which it was made. Or it may be the quiet discovery that one does not need to go somewhere, with chariots, or ships, or feet, or wings, since God is more truly like our spirits than like anything else in the universe, not remote, or absentee, close as breathing the normal environment of the soul, and therefore a real Presence to be found and known and loved, as the swimmer finds the ocean. And this attitude of faith may rise, as it does with me in my best and sanest moments, to a joyous consciousness of acquaintance, fellowship, and love. Sometimes it is a flash of sudden insight, sometimes it is a quiet assurance, sometimes it is an unspeakable joy in living, sometimes it is a dim awareness of a resource to live by and to draw upon for action.

It brings a sense of "at homeness" in this strange world. Nobody ever said this better than did that great mystic who wrote the "blessing of Moses" in Deuteronomy: "The eternal God is our home and underneath us are the everlasting arms." It is the consciousness of "Belonging," of being "no longer strangers and sojourners," as St. Paul discovered, "but fellow-citizens with the saints in the household of God... builded together into a temple for the habitation of God in the Spirit...."

The true secret seems to be found in the closing of chasms and cleavages. The divided will, the divided mind, the divided heart, become fused into a unity. The antithetic parts of the self, which were in a state of civil war, become one harmonious whole. The entire inner being ceases its usual crossroad dilemmas and goes in one direction, straight forward. But even more important than this healing of inward breaches in the soul is the discovery of the conjunctness of God and man in a union of love and fellowship above all divisions. The divided life, the sundered self, the isolated ego, cannot be at peace. It cannot be "saved" in any true sense, while it is away from home in a far country on the other side of a wide canyon of separation from God. Nobody ever saw that truth more clearly than St. Paul did. "Saw" it is the right word, for what men usually call his "theology," his "system," was first of all an experience in life. He vividly saw and felt. To read forensic theological theories into Paul's throbbing letters is to miss the main artery by which he lived.

His doctrine of salvation is the outgrowth of his own personal experience of a mystic union through Christ, a union which does away with the "middle wall of partition" and brings together in an at-onement of reconciliation the two that were before separated by a chasm. "It is no longer I (the separate ego)," he says in one of his most striking autobiographical passages, "that live, but Christ liveth in me (by a mystical union), and the life I now live in the flesh I live in faith, the faith which is in the Son of God who loved me and gave himself for me." Here in this marvelous experience of union through love, one finds himself in the sphere of life, not in the realm of logical theory.   — TL 192–97

TWO PATHS

There are two very diverse types of mystical attitude which come out of the testimony of consciousness to the soul's relation to God. I shall call the two classes, respectively, "negation mysticism" and "affirmation mysticism," though these words are used merely for purposes of description.

Negation Mysticism. The sense of the divine presence will naturally work very different results upon different persons. If one discovers that he is a partaker of the divine life, what shall he do next? Why, answers the mystic of our first class, he shall make it his goal to become absorbed in God — swallowed up in the Godhead.

Where can God be found? Not in our world of sense anywhere, answers this mystic. Every possible object in our world is a mere finite appearance. It may be as huge as the sun or even the Milky Way, or as minute as the dust speck in the sunbeam; it makes no difference. It is a form of finitude. It is, in contrast to the Absolute, an illusion, a thing of unreality. It cannot show God or take you to Him.

No better is the situation when you can fix upon some event of history or some deed of a person in his social relations. The event is a mere finite fact. Cut off and treated by itself, it is not a true reality. God cannot be found in it. The same thing applies to inner states. They are no better than finite activities. Every state of consciousness is sadly finite. It always seeks a beyond. Consciousness is the symbol of restlessness. It is like the flight of the bird which has not found its nest. When the soul is perfectly at home in God, all thought will be quenched, all consciousness will cease.

"Believe not," cries one of these mystics, "those prattlers who boast that they know God. Who knows Him — is silent." He proceeds therefore by process of negation. Everything finite must be transcended. He must slough off not only the rags of his own righteousness, but the last vestige of his finitude. Union with God, absorption in His Being, so that "self" and "other" are unknown is the goal of his search:

> *Some little talk awhile of Me and Thee*
> *There was — and then no more of Thee and Me.*

He is seeking for an immediate experience which shall fulfill every finite purpose and leave nothing to be sought or desired — a now that shall hint of no beyond. One sees that this mystic is asking for something which cannot be granted, or at least for something which could not be known if it were attained. The Absolute who is postulated as precisely the negation of all finiteness turns out to be for us mortals only an absolute zero — a limitless sum-total of negation....

One sees at once the logical and practical outcome of the mysticism of negation. It ends in contraction and confusion or at least would so end if the person were faithful to his principle. "It is," as one of our rare American teachers has said, "as if the bud, knowing that its life is in the life of the parent tree, should seek to become one with the tree by withering and shrinking and letting its life ebb back into the common life. Seeing it we should not say, Behold how this bud has become one with the tree; we should say, The bud is dead."

Then, too, it has been the tendency of this type of mysticism to encourage men to live for the rare moment of ecstasy and beatific vision, to sacrifice the chance of winning spiritual victory for the hope of receiving an ineffable illumination which would quench all further search or desire.

Affirmation Mysticism. We turn now to the affirmation mystics. They do not make vision the end of life, but rather the beginning. They are bent on having an immediate, firsthand sense of God — but not just for the joy of having it. More important than vision is obedience to the vision. There are battles to fight and victories to win. God's Kingdom is to be advanced. Error is to be attacked and truth to be established. Those who would have a closer view of the Divine must seek it in a life of love and sacrifice.

Instead of seeking the Absolute by negating the finite, the mystic of this class finds the revelation of God *in* the finite.

Nothing now can be unimportant. There is more in the least
event than the ordinary eye sees. Every situation may be turned
into an occasion for winning a nearer view of God. The most
stubborn fact which fronts one in the path may be made a revelation of divine glory, for to this mystic every finite fact may
become an open window into the Divine.

It is a primary fact for him that he partakes of God, that
his being comes out of the life of God and that he is never beyond the reach of God Who is his source. But this true being
is to be wrought out in the world where he can know only
finite and imperfect things. His mission on earth is to be a
fellow worker with God — contributing in a normal daily life
his human powers to the divine Spirit who works in him and
about him, bringing to reality a kingdom of God.

His life with its plainly visible tasks is always like the pa-
limpsest which bears in underlying writing a sacred text. He is
always more than any finite task declares, and yet he accepts
this task because he has discovered that only *through* the finite is the Infinite to be found. His mystical insight gives him
a unity which does not lie beyond the transitory and temporal,
but which includes them and gives them their reality. The slenderest human task becomes glorious because God is in it. The
simplest act of duty is good because it makes the Infinite God
more real. The slightest deed of pure love is a holy thing because
God shines through it and is revealed by it.

It is because beauty is a unity that any beautiful object whatever may suffice to show it and any object that does show it
has an opening into the infinite. It is because God is a complete
unity that any being who partakes of Him may in measure manifest Him. The whole purpose of the one who holds this view is
to make his life the best possible organ of God.

He too, like our other mystics, seeks union with God, but
not through loss of personality. The eye serves the body not by

extinguishing itself but by increasing its power of discrimination; so too the soul is ever more one with the Lord of life as it identifies itself with Him and lets His being expand its human powers....

The prayer of the affirmation mystic will be:

> *Leave me not, God, until — nay, until when?*
> *Not till I am with thee, one heart, one mind;*
> *Not till thy life is light in me, and then*
> *Leaving is left behind.*
>
> — SL 131–33, 134–37, 138

THE MYSTICAL ELEMENT IN PRIMITIVE CHRISTIANITY

The great epochs in religion, and particularly this greatest epoch, which we call the "apostolic age," are marked off and characterized by a peculiarly rich and vivid consciousness of the divine presence. They are times when in new, fresh, and transforming ways persons have *experienced* the real presence of God. Life is always raised to new levels, and receives a new dynamic quality whenever God becomes real in personal and social experience. The battle has raged long and bitterly over the metaphysical relation of Christ to God; great rallying cries have grown out of these battles, and different communions have gathered about the various formulations of doctrine upon these and other difficult metaphysical questions, but the much more important questions are questions of fact — namely, what were the significant features of Christ's experience, what gave Him His extraordinary power over those who were in fellowship with Him, and what was it that made His disciples in such ef-

fective ways "the salt of the earth, the light of the world" —
and these questions have hardly been raised at all.

The time is coming, however, when the emphasis will shift —
it is already shifting — from questions of systematic theology
to questions of religious experience, from metaphysics to psychology. It is a point of the first importance that the Gospels
have given us little or no metaphysics; the language of theology is, too, quite foreign to them. They have given us instead
the portrait of a Person who had a most extraordinary experience of God and of Oneness with Him. We may wish that we
had more of the very words of this Person, and that our accounts of His life were not colored by His reporters; but we
ought rather to be grateful that these first-century biographers
have, with unstudied simplicity, given us so little of themselves,
and have opened to us so many approaches to the real life and
even the actual consciousness of the Person who originated in
the world this new and intimate fellowship with God which we
call Christianity.

We should be very far from depreciating the impressive
efforts of scholars, ancient and modern, to gather up and for-
mulate the teaching of Jesus, the original message, for no one
can fail to recognize that He was a Master, that He taught
disciples, and that His teachings, His dominant ideas, have
enormously influenced human thought, and have formed a large
factor in the moral evolution of the race; but no summary
of Christ's teachings, no formulation of His dominant ideas,
can give us a full account of primitive Christianity, for primitive Christianity is supremely this unique Person, Jesus Christ,
with His experience of God, His insight into the meaning of
Life, His consecration to the task of remaking man, and the
extraordinary fellowship which His Spirit produced.

Christianity in the golden age was essentially a rich and vivid
consciousness of God, rising to a perfect experience of union

with God in mind and heart and will. It was a personal exhibition of the Divine in the human, the Eternal in the midst of time. When we get back to the head-waters of our religion, we come ultimately to a Person who felt, and, in childlike simplicity, said, that "No man knows the Father save the Son," and "I and the Father are one."

The direct impact and power of His life on His followers is the most extraordinary thing in the Gospels, and the continued power of His life over men is the most marvelous thing in human history. The source of this power is to be found in the fact that men have found through Him a direct way to God, that by His life and death they have been drawn themselves into a personal experience of God in some degree like His own. He always taught His disciples to expect this, and it was their attainment of this experience that made them the apostles of the new religion. Christianity is thus at its very heart a mystical religion — a religion which lives and flourishes because its members experience what its Founder experienced, the actual presence of God as the formative Spirit of a new creation. As I have said, every disciple was summoned to expect a direct and conscious incoming of the divine life. "Wherever two or three are gathered in My name, there am I in the midst" (Matt. 18:20), was the announcement of a mystical fellowship which has cheered the hearts of little groups of worshipers in all ages and in all lands where the words of the Gospel have come. "Lo, I am with you always" was a promise which fed and watered the faith of men in the hard days of cross and stake, and in the long, uneventful years when no "sign" was given that the fellowship of the saints would finally overcome the world.

The members of this primitive group were taught in the most impressive way to avoid anxiety and worry, and, instead, to open their souls to the circulation of divine forces of life which build up the inward life as noiselessly and yet as beautifully as the lily's robe is spun and the cubits are added to the carefree child. They were told not to be disturbed about their defense before judges and authorities in times of strait, but to trust to the springs of wisdom that would flow into them from the larger Life of the Holy Spirit in which they lived. The promise of direct and inward fellowship with Christ took on wider scope, according to the recently discovered "saying" of Jesus, "Wherever any man raises a stone or cleaves wood, there am I"; for whether this is a genuine saying of Jesus, or an early Christian reminiscence of an idea which He taught in a more general way, it undoubtedly expresses in graphic language one of the deepest truths which pervade the original teaching, namely, that the disciple, whether gathered for worship or defending himself before the authorities, or engaged in simple labor with his hands, is to share a direct fellowship with Christ, a fellowship which shall consecrate every spot of the earth and hallow every occupation.

The pictorial description of the Judgment Day identifies God with the least member of the mystical fellowship. There is no other passage in the New Testament which announces more positively the solidarity of the race and the conjunct life of God and man. He, the Head of the Fellowship, drinks of the cup put to the lips of the thirsty child, and the slenderest ministry performed out of love circulates through the whole, and touches the infinite Heart (Matt. 25:31–46). This description ought to have softened the lurid colors which have so often been used to paint the Judgment Day — supposed to be a *dies irae;* but there is unmistakable evidence that the idea of the solidarity of humanity, the announcement that God identifies Himself with the hungry and naked and persecuted — even the least — the teaching that every man in the deeps of his soul is bound in with God, which are expressed in this primitive narrative, have exercised a marked influence on those groups of Christians who have gone to the Gospel itself for their illumination.

The entire teaching of the Kingdom of God has its mystical aspect. It is a society, or fellowship, both in earth and in heaven, both human and divine. Its capital is not in some foreign land, its King is not a distant Sovereign, for any member of the Kingdom at any spot of earth can see Him if his heart is pure. The person who belongs to the Kingdom is a person in whom God lives and rules, and through whom the contagion of a love, caught from above, spreads through the world. The Kingdom is the life of God exhibited in human fellowship, the heavenly life appearing here in the midst of time, the sway of God in human hearts; it is a human society which grows on and flowers out and ripens its fruit, because its unseen roots are in God the Life.

Instead of founding a Church in the technical sense, Christ brought a little group of men and women into a personal experience of God, similar to His own, and left them baptized in a consciousness of the Spirit's presence to form the Church as the conditions and demands of different epochs and diverse lands should require. "I give unto you the keys," is said not only to Peter, but to every disciple who has reached the insight, not by flesh and blood, but by spiritual perception, that Christ is the son of the living God — the personal realization of the life of God in a human life.

The Church itself, then, as seen in its simplest conception, is a mystical fellowship, formed and gathered not by the will of man, nor schemes of flesh and blood, but by direct revelation from God to the soul. The first spiritual stone in the structure, which is to defy time and death, is a person who is chosen because by revelation he has discovered the Divine in the human; and with only one stone ready, Christ sees the spiritual building of the ages rising and reaching beyond the power of death. Each believer is a mystical stone. To each person who lives by his faith and vision of the Son of God the key is given. In a word, the authority is within the spiritual soul, and not external to it. Each member is crowned and mitred.

The primitive Church, in its first stage, as it is described in Acts, was clearly a mystical fellowship, i.e., a fellowship bound together, not by external organization, but by the power of the experience of the divine presence among the members. It is evident that many were drawn into the fellowship by their expectation of an imminent return of the Christ who, they believed, had disappeared for an interval, and would come soon to restore all things and to give the Kingdom to Israel. But it is just as evident that there was at least a nucleus of persons in the group who were recipients of first-hand experiences of an extraordinary sort, and who lived, not on expectation, but on the actual experience of unwonted spiritual visitation.

At this stage of Christian consciousness the Holy Spirit was thought of as a power coming from without into the person. The divine incoming was conceived as an invasion — as a mighty rushing wind — and the effects looked for were miraculous, sudden, and temporary. The little group which gathered from house to house, eating their bread together in gladness and singleness of heart, lived in the borderland of ecstasy and exhibited the extraordinary phenomena which have appeared in some measure wherever mystical groups have been formed. Speaking with tongues was not confined to the one occasion when the little band felt the inrushing of the mighty wind. It was common in the primitive Church, and seems to have appeared wherever the first Christians went. Paul treats it in Corinthians as though it were a regular gift, which was to be looked for whenever the Spirit came upon men. The atmosphere was charged with wonder, and men expected incursions from the unseen world into the sphere of their daily lives.

There can be no question that these simple and unstudied accounts of the life of the primitive fellowship have played a great role in the history of the Church. The fellowship itself, with all things in common, the agape or love feast, the consciousness of divine invasion, the expectation of the marvelous, the unconcern about the affairs of this life, the experiment to form a society governed from within and guided by ecstatic prophecy, have been in some degree repeated again and again. The duration of the primitive fellowship, at least in its simple and mystical form, was short. The Jerusalem Church was soon organized under a visible head — James, the brother of the Lord — and the whole basis of the Church life and polity was powerfully affected by the remarkable missionary activity of Paul, and by the proclamation of what he himself called his "Gospel."   —MR 3–9

FINDING SELF, FINDING GOD

I am not interested in mysticism as an "ism." It turns out in most accounts to be a dry and abstract thing, hardly more like the warm and intimate experience than the color of a map is like the country for which it stands. "Canada is very pink," seems quite an inadequate description of the noble country north of our border. It is mystical experience and not mysticism that is worthy of our study. We are concerned with the experience itself, not with secondhand formulations of it. "The mystic," says Professor [Josiah] Royce, "is a thorough-going empiricist." "God ceases to be an object and becomes an experience," says Professor [Andrew] Pringle-Pattison. If it is an experience, we want to find out what happens to the mystic himself inside where he lives. According to those who have been there the experience which we call mystical is charged with the conviction of real, direct contact and commerce with God. It is the almost universal testimony of those who are mystics that they find God through their experience. John Tauler says that in his best moments of "devout prayer and the uplifting of the mind to God," he experiences the "pure presence of God in his own soul," but he adds that all he can tell others about the experience is "as poor and unlike it as the point of a needle is to the heavens above us." "I have met with my God; I have met with my Savior. I have felt the healings drop upon my soul from under His wings," says Isaac Penington in the joy of his first mystical experience. Without needlessly multiplying such testimonies for data, we can say with considerable assurance that mystical experience is consciousness of direct and immediate relationship with some transcendent reality which in the moment of experience is believed to be God. "This is He, this is He," exclaims Isaac Penington, "there is no other: This is He whom I have waited for and sought after from my childhood." Angela of Foligno says that she experienced God, and saw that the whole world was full of God.

There are many different degrees of intensity, concentration, and conviction in the experiences of different individual mystics, and also in the various experiences of the same individual from time to time. There has been a tendency in most studies of mysticism to regard the state of ecstasy as par excellence mystical experience. That is, however, a grave mistake. The calmer, more meditative, less emotional, less ecstatic experiences of God are not less convincing and possess greater constructive value for life and character than do ecstatic experiences which presuppose a peculiar psychical frame and disposition. The seasoned Quaker in the corporate hush and stillness of a silent meeting is far removed from ecstasy, but he is not the less convinced that he is meeting with God. For the essence of mysticism we do not need to insist upon a certain "sacred" mystic way nor upon ecstasy, nor upon any peculiar type of rare psychic upheavals. We do need to insist, however, upon a consciousness of commerce with God amounting to conviction of his presence.

Jacob Boehme calls the experience which came to him, "breaking through the gate," into "a new birth or resurrection from the dead," so that, he says, "I knew God." "I am certain," says [Meister] Eckhart, "as certain as that I live, that nothing is so near to me as God. God is nearer to me than I am to myself." One of these experiences — the first one — was an ecstasy, and the other, so far as we can tell, was not. It was the flooding in of a moment of God-consciousness in the act of preaching a sermon to the common people of Cologne. The experience of Penington again, was not an ecstasy; it was the vital surge of fresh life on the first occasion of hearing George Fox preach after a long period of waiting silence.... Brother Lawrence, a barefooted lay brother of the seventeenth century, according to the testimony of the brotherhood, attained "an unbroken and undisturbed sense of the Presence of God." He was not an ecstatic; he was a quiet, faithful man who did his ordinary daily tasks with what seemed to his friends "an unclouded vision, an illuminated love and an uninterrupted joy." Simple and humble though he was, he nevertheless acquired, through his experience of God, "an extraordinary spaciousness of mind."

The more normal, expansive mystical experiences come apparently when the personal self is at its best. Its powers and capacities are raised to an unusual unity and fused together. The whole being, with its accumulated submerged life, *finds itself.* The process of preparing for any high achievement is a severe and laborious one, but nothing seems easier in the moment of success than is the accomplishment for which the life has been prepared. There comes to be formed within the person what Aristotle called "a dexterity of soul," so that the person does with ease what he has become skilled to do. Clement of Alexandria called a fully organized and spiritualized person "a harmonized man," that is, adjusted, organized, and ready to be a transmissive organ for the revelation of God. Brother Lawrence, who was thus "harmonized," finely says: "The most excellent method which I found of going to God was that of doing my common business, purely for the love of God." An earlier mystic of the fourteenth century stated the same principle in these words: "It is my aim to be to the Eternal God what a man's hand is to a man."

There are many human experiences which carry a man up to levels where he has not usually been before and where he finds himself possessed of insight and energies he had hardly suspected were his until that moment. One leaps to his full height when the right inner spring is reached. We are quite familiar with the way in which instinctive tendencies in us and emotions both egoistic and social, become organized under a group of ideas and ideals into a single system which we call a sentiment, such as love, or patriotism, or devotion to truth. It forms slowly and one hardly realizes that it has formed until some occasion unexpectedly brings it into full operation, and we find ourselves able with perfect ease to overcome the most powerful inhibitory and opposing instincts and habits, which, until then, had usually controlled us. We are familiar, too, with the way in which a well-trained and disciplined mind, confronted by a concrete situation, will sometimes — alas, not always — in a sudden flash of imaginative insight, discover a universal law revealed there and then in the single phenomenon. . . . Literary and artistic geniuses supply us with many instances in which, in a sudden flash, the crude material at hand is shot through with vision and the complicated plot of a drama, the full significance of a character, or the complete glory of a statue stands revealed. . . .

There is a famous account of the flash of inspiration given by Philo, which can hardly be improved. It is as follows: "I am not ashamed to recount my own experience. At times, when I have proposed to enter upon my wonted task of writing on philosophical doctrines, with an exact knowledge of the materials which were to be put together, I have had to leave off without any work accomplished, finding my mind barren and fruitless, and upbraiding it for its self-complacency, while startled at the might of the Existent One, in whose power it lies to open and close the wombs of the soul. But at other times, when I had come empty, all of a sudden I have been filled with thoughts, showered down and sown upon me unseen from above, so that by divine possession I have fallen into a rapture and become ignorant of everything, the place, those present, myself, what was spoken or written. For I have received a stream of interpretation, a fruition of light, the most clear-cut sharpness of vision, the most vividly distinct view of the matter before me, such as might be received through the eyes from the most luminous presentation."

The most important mystical experiences are something like that. They occur usually not at the beginning of the religious life but rather in the ripe and developed stage of it. They are the fruit of long-maturing processes. Clement's "the harmonized man" is always a person who has brought his soul into parallelism with divine currents, has habitually practiced his religious insights, and has finally formed a unified central self, subtly sensitive, acutely responsive to the Beyond within him. In such experiences, which may come suddenly or may come as a more gradual process, the whole self operates and masses all the culminations of a lifetime. They are no more emotional than they are rational and volitional. We have a total personality, awake, active, and "aware of his life's flow." Instead of seeing in a flash a law of gravitation, or the plot of Hamlet, or the uncarved form of Moses the Law-giver in a block of marble, one sees at such times the moral demonstrations of a lifetime and vividly feels the implications that are essentially involved in a spiritual life. In the high moment God is seen to be as sure as the soul is.

To some the truth of God never comes closer than a logical conclusion. He is held to be as a living item in a creed. To the mystic he becomes real in the same sense that experienced beauty is real, or the feel of spring is real, or that summer sunlight is real — he has been found, he has been met, he is present.

— SE 135–44

THE FEEL OF OBJECTIVITY

It remains for us to consider the important question of the verification of mystical experience. How do we know that the mystic's experience is not a blind trail, a mere "projection" of his subjective longings? May it not be an unconscious extension of that amazing capacity in us for "auto-suggestion"? In the first place, it should be pointed out... that "projection" and "auto-suggestion" are abnormal, pathological phenomena and that it is not legitimate to use these terms in connection with religious experiences which are the highest indications of health and normality. It is true, however, that powers of mind which have come to light in pathological cases may also have important constructive functions in processes of great importance for life values. There can be no doubt, I think, that auto-suggestion in the good sense is always operating and carrying us forward with prevision of ideal possibilities and even "projection," as a forecast of what ought to be, may have its place in the normal healthy activities of life.

It is enough in any case to insist here that there is no good ground or reason for using pathological terms to bring the mystic's experiences into disrepute or for putting them into a class with dreams as though they were mental "constructions," unless the experiences themselves bear the well-known stigmata of pathological phenomena. Some of the experiences of mystics do and some of them do not show such marks. I shall proceed to deal with experiences that seem as normal as breathing and which manifestly add to the whole dynamic quality of life — its power to stand the universe and to remake it nearer to the heart's desire. William James said of Ignatius Loyola that "his mysticism made him assuredly one of the most powerfully practical human engines that ever lived." That statement can fairly and truthfully be made regarding a long list of mystics. St. Bernard of Clairvaux and George Fox are two good specimens of this heightened moral, spiritual, and practical power, released and set into action by a personal experience of God present in their lives. In fact mystics as a class of men and women have not only been saints, they have been girded for action through their contact with God and they have exhibited indomitable spirit and energy for constructive tasks. They have revealed serenity, sanity, and sound capacity for leadership and cooperation with others. Auto-suggestion and projection in the pathological sense do not lead to such results. They lead to ineffectiveness and futility.

It should be noted that there is a school of psychologists who state with unqualified emphasis that there can be but one pathway to reality and that is the way of the special senses. If an experience cannot be traced to a definite peripheral origin in sense, they would say, it may be discounted at once as a dream, a fancy, a projection. In no case can it ever bring truth or enlarge our acquaintance with the universe in which we live. Those who speak that way belong, however, with the dogmatists, not with the sound investigators of truth. They assert what nobody has proved or can prove and they weaken the whole strength of their authoritative pronouncement by failing to give any sufficient or convincing explanation of sense-experience as a way of knowledge. In the last analysis even in their accounts it turns out to be as miraculous as Aladdin's palace. You rub a retina with ether-vibrations and lo, you see, not ether, but truth. You surge waves through the organ of Corti in the inner ear and presto, you know a fact of spiritual moment. You touch finger-tips against a certain physical substance and behold, you have a piece of momentous information. If ever there was a mystery, there it is! It may be true, of course, that all knowledge must have some sense-factor to it, but we must know vastly more about the nature of sense-factors than we do now before we dare assert even that with finality. What I am insisting upon is that the mind of man is an immense activity and it, in its totality, with its innate dispositions, is behind and in every experience which leads to truth, and we have not fathomed yet its range or scope.

What we must tie to as a guiding principle is the fact or feeling of objectivity which attaches to our cognitive experience, i.e., our knowledge-bringing experience. We know it to be utterly different from our dreams, our fancies, our subjective longings. It comes to us with a certainty that what we perceive is *there*, that it is not in our mind, or projected out from our minds, into space, but is in its own right *real* — a true object. We have tests for its reality. We try it by our other senses. We get the testimony of other persons — the group-test. We measure it; we photograph it and so on, but all the time we build upon and stake our life upon the testimony of our minds to objectivity. It is again in the last resort a mystery, but there it is and we rest the pillars of the world upon it.

Mystical experiences of the important and constructive type have this same feeling of objectivity. They do not bear the mark of dreams or fancies; they bear all the signs and evidences of something really *there*. It is true that this objectivity cannot be tested precisely as we test sense-objects. We cannot call our friend and ask him if he finds the real presence of God where we are sure that we have found it. We are compelled to turn for evidence now to moral and spiritual effects which attend the conviction or we must ask our friend to go through the discipline and preparation through which we have passed to see if a similar experience may not break through upon him. But there is no denying that we are moving now in another field from that of sense-facts and we cannot get the same coefficients and common denominators that mark our group experience in the well-known frame-works of space and time. We must content ourselves with the coercive feeling of objectivity and with the public demonstration which the fruits of the transformed and fortified life furnish. What men, who have had the contact with God, do with their lives, what they suffer for love's sake, what they endure for the truth which they have seen, is the surest evidence we can produce in support of the fact that they themselves have the conviction of objectivity. Their heightened effectiveness, their increased capacity as "human engines," their unique power of leadership and of carrying their vision into practical, social operation in the world around them is the best proof which can be adduced for the belief that there *is* some objective reality to their experience, that it is not *maya* and illusion.

I have discussed in another place the part which conation, i.e., tendencies and disposition toward effort and action, play in all our systems of belief and in all our estimates of truth. There are within us certain native strivings, urges, tropes, dispositions to activity, and these are governing forces in every intellectual process of human life, and it may well be that St. Augustine is right in that greatest saying of his, "Thou, O God, hast made us for Thyself and we are restless until we find our rest in Thee." It may be that with man there has come this new and strange emergence, a native longing and disposition for God, for the deeper World from which we have come, and that may be the basis of all real religion, and this tendency, which reaches the flowering point in mystics, may be a true sign of our spiritual lineage as well as of our spiritual destiny.

By far the larger number of mystics probably live and die without explicitly knowing that they *are* mystics. They are active conative mystics rather than cognitive mystics. They practice the presence of God instead of arriving at a clear state of knowledge about it. They do not point to some moment when they could say with Isaac Penington, "I have met with my God." They quietly manifest in acts that energies not their own and incursions of power from beyond themselves are coming through them. . . . This may well be called "practical mysticism," or as I have named it, "conative-mysticism" — mysticism of life and action. It is the greatest kind there is and its power in any given life is cumulative. It gathers momentum and force like a rolling snowball.   — FE 111–16

3

Christ's Body, God's Kingdom

For Christians, Jesus is the perfect example of a soul totally open to God in mystical communion. Jesus is the vibrantly living sign of the Infinite's presence in the finite as well as a reminder of the destiny to which each of us is called. As John's Gospel says, Jesus is the "truth" — truth as a transformative experience of the God-saturated universe. When we embrace that truth, we cleave more intimately to the divine environment in which we dwell. We participate in Christ.

Jones believes that genuine participation in Christ's life, ministry, and resurrection is possible only within the context of the "beloved community." This community, the Body of Christ, is the "living expression and growing interpretation in the world of the mind and spirit of Christ." "In the world": Christ's body is here and now, growing the eternal in the soil of time and fertilizing it with divine love, leading each of us ever deeper into one another's and God's heart. Membership in the beloved community enables us to participate in the divine giving, sharing, and loving exemplified by Christ. Its growth rate, and ours, is slow and steady, as all genuine growth is. But the fruits are a deeper fellowship with both our brothers and sisters and with God — an expansive enrichment that Jones calls "living to live" — wherein

*our souls so open to the Divine that we utterly fulfill our natures
as creatures made by and for God. To abide and labor in the
Body of Christ, to "go the second mile," is to edge toward that
perfect union of spirit and Spirit — the heavenly Kingdom — for
which the whole universe groans and travails. The selections in
this chapter eloquently speak to this grand vision.*

CHRIST IS OURS

A major question is whether the coming of Christ can be
thought of as a historical event or not. Does Christ belong to
history, or is He beyond history? Is His coming a watershed in
history, or does He stand entirely apart from history? Does He
come in a wholly perpendicular direction, as a celestial visitant
from another realm, entering our world from beyond, breaking
in on it from another sphere, and then leaving it again when the
brief span of His work on earth was finished? Both views have
been held and still are held today.

If one begins with the assumption that human nature is spiritually sterile and in dualistic fashion wholly sundered from
God, and the historical process is wholly horizontal and devoid of correspondence with an internal environment, then the
only conceivable way for Christ, or any revealer of the Eternal, to come to our world as a divine event, as a revelation
of God, would be for Him to come perpendicularly from beyond the time-world, to remain apart while here, and to have
no historical correlation with the normal currents of life and
history before and after. This view that Christ was a stupen-
dous injection into the world from beyond, uncorrelated with
history, and without being contaminated by contact with life
here below, leads very easily on into "docetism," which was serious heresy in the early Church. Those who were determined

to maintain that Christ was absolutely divine and wholly other than man went to the extreme position of insisting that Christ's earthly birth and temptation and suffering and death were only "seemings," "presentations of ideas made visible and vocal to men's minds." He never actually shared in the common experiences of human life, and He never really entered this stream of human events. His coming was an instance of "misplaced concreteness."

To set Christ out of relation with human life and with history, to put Him in unique isolation, either ends in some form of docetism, or at best turns Him into a mysterious being who moves so far above the life we know and share that He does not bring a real redemptive power to bear on us. Everything ends for us in unreality. This extreme type of interpretation has almost invariably resulted in producing a violent swing of the pendulum off to the other extreme, and there emerges an emphasis on the purely human aspect of Christ. The difficulty throughout has been due to a misreading of human life. If man were wholly separated from God, depraved in nature, and spiritually sterile, there could be no real incarnation in such a being as that. And in following the shifts and make-shifts to which theological interpreters have resorted, one can see through it all that the impasse is made by a false and unsound theory of man.

If, as I am convinced is the case, man is essentially related to God, created in His image, and never sundered from the deeper world of Spirit; if the time-stream itself is embedded in the deeps of Eternity and expresses reality "splashed out" into succession, and if history as a living movement is under the guiding, steering hand of a Pilot, who in spite of the zig-zags, goes forward toward a goal, then it would not be utterly impossible to think of Christ as revealing the full significance of Life and History and as a revelation of the direction in which man ought to move. Then the *preparatio evangelica*, the slow stages of prepa-

ration for the event, would all be significant and full of real
meaning, which otherwise they lack. I know as well as anybody
does how sinful man is, what a poor, pitiable thing he can be.
But I insist that that is not the whole story. There is some un-
lost likeness in man to which God can appeal, and we somehow
feel that "Christ is ours," and "we belong." Men's faith, their
spiritual outlook, their interpretation of the significance of life,
have always been important factors in the shaping of history. In
other words, the spiritual element has been all the way along a
determining feature of the historical process.

I find an Eternal Gospel of the Spirit dimly breaking through
the time-stream in many ways. I think of man in all his devious
wanderings in far countries as a possible child of God, who is
never too remote to hear authentic tidings of Home and Father,
and who has actually progressed in the long upward journey.
Christ is what we should expect at some stage of history. . . .

At the head-waters of the stream of Christianity we come
upon a Person who exhibited in matchless degree the divine
possibilities of our kind of life and who was in a most exalted sense a revealing center of that deeper divine life that is
within the reach of us all. In him both worlds were together in
unity. He participated in Eternity. He revealed divine grace as
no else has done. He was a genuinely historical person, living
connected with the past and with the future. But no account
of him in terms of pedigree, or background, or of country, or
national traits, or of social-group influences, or of nurture, or
Zeitgeist, will ever explain him. He is unique. He transcends all
the known frontiers and boundaries. He shares in many of the
ideas and in the outlooks and expectations of the time. But he
is always far beyond them. One can see the lines of the influence of the past in much that he said and did. The prophets
and the apocalyptists left their stamp on him. But he was always on ahead of their highest point. The gates of the future

always stood open before him. If he winnows and gathers up the seed-thought of the past, he just as certainly anticipates the spiritual discoveries of unborn generations. It fills one with awe and wonder to see how his truth and wisdom and spiritual insight outstrip the stock of the ages behind him and move on ahead of the foremost files of after generations. He brought and continues to bring a new quality of life into humanity.

His life, his spirit, his personality, is incomparably greater than anything he said, or did, or taught. One is always aware that there is more where his words come from. He is there all the time above and beyond his utterances. It was a remarkable stroke of insight that led St. John to declare that he was the *truth*. Truth as it is used here is not a logical judgment, or a spoken message, or a transmitted idea; it is something that a person can be. It is a *life* that corresponds with an ideal, a pattern, an architectural plan. A person has come at last who can be the way, the truth, and the life....

What Christ brought to light in the unfolding of the Eternal Gospel is the Face, the personal aspect, the revelation of the Heart, the Love, the Grace, the Character-Nature, of God. We *see* Him at last. We know now what He is like. We are confined no longer to abstract attributes, such as "infinite," "omniscient," "omnipotent," and "absolute." We come closer into the Heart of things and find that the highest and most exalted Being is our Father, who had all along been seeking us while we were feeling our way to Him.   —EG 88–91, 97–101

BELOVED COMMUNITY

There is only a tiny fraction of truth in any attempt to reduce religion to what one does alone with God in one's solitariness. The primary fact of human life is not the lonely individual, but the group that makes the individual possible. There can be no self emerge in this world without a mother, without a purveyor of food; there can be no acquisition of language, no nurture of mind or spirit, no formation of ideals, no basis of reality without some kind of background society. Society of some sort is the primitive fact. One person alone is simply nobody at all. An isolated being with no relationships would be more difficult to find than the missing link, and when found would contribute nothing to the meaning of life. Only in a madhouse can one find a completely isolated self....

Religion, which is as immemorial as smiling and weeping, does not begin with a St. Stylites alone on the top of a pillar. If it had so begun the saint would soon have perished without a sympathetic community to see him — or what is more important, to admire him. It is foolish for us to waste any precious time trying to settle the issue whether religion originates with the individual or the group. It is as absurd as trying to find a stick which has only one end. Individual and group cannot be cut apart and be treated as though either were real as a sundered existent.

The moment an individual has arrived on the scene with a capacity for the mystical, that is, the direct personal apprehension of God and capacity to interpret his experience, there is bound to be behind this individual the long molding processes of history, the accumulations of the experiences and transmissions of many generations. If the given individual runs on ahead of the group, as a prophet-genius does, it will be along the lines and in the direction for which the group has long been preparing the line of march. And the individual does not possess his insight with a permanent assurance until he has interpreted it and carried others along with this conviction. In short, however important the creative insight of the rare soul may be, religion does not count as a contribution to the race until a beloved community is formed and the discovery is interpreted and transmuted into a social movement. As far as its significance is concerned, religion is essentially social. It is an affair of a beloved community.

St. Paul was not exaggerating when he declared that the church-group is Christ's body — the new body which is to be the living expression and growing interpretation in the world of the mind and spirit of Christ through the ages. And St. John is only stating what was literally the truth when he has Christ say of the new fellowship, "I am the vine-stock and you are the vine-branches of one living organism." There never was a time when Christianity was a disembodied idea, or ideal, or spirit. The Gospel itself was formulated and came to the world through the beloved community, and Christianity has always lived on and has always been transmitted through the Body of believers we call the Church.

I mean, then, by "the Church," the Body of Christian believers and transmitters of Christ's mind and spirit through the centuries, rather than a specific organization, or institution, or a single concrete communion, however extensive or historically important. This larger, all-inclusive body of believers has sometimes been called the Church Universal, or what the spiritual reformers in the sixteenth century called the "Invisible Church," or in St. Augustine's famous phrase the *Civitas dei qualis nunc in terra* — the City of God as it now is on earth.

This continuous unbroken invisible Church of the Ages as the total Body of Believers has always been a social and socializing force in the world. It has always expressed its truth, its spiritual message, in terms of a society. Its saints have not usually been "exhibits" on lonely pillars; they have been men and women living in the world and expressing in life and action the ideals of their faith as they held it at the time. The Church has always been a society of people living in the midst of the world, pene-

trated by certain convictions about life. Even in periods when
no one yet talked of a "social gospel" in the modern sense,
Christianity was nevertheless an immense constructive and socializing force in the reconstruction of the Western World after
the overthrow of the Roman Empire by the hordes of the bar-
barian invaders. The *Civitas dei* went right on as an operative
power when the visible empire was submerged, and built the
new epoch....

The Church of the Ages is a stream which began in mighty
Head-waters, and it has until today kept its onward flow more
or less influenced on great occasions by its fontal tides of the
Spirit. It can continue its mission, its divine function in the
world, only as it discovers how to minister in some adequate
way both to the souls and the bodies of men. There can be no
significant continuing Church, which is concerned solely with
what is to happen eschatologically in a post-mortem sphere beyond the glimpses of the moon. The Church must face the real
issues of life and make a practical difference in the lives of actual men and women and children, or it is doomed to become a
disappearing affair. That does not mean that it is to become secularized. A completely secularized Church has already reached
its terminus, and its mission as a Church of Christ is over.

The primary function of a Church, if it is to be a continuing
Body of Christ in the world, is to raise human life out of its
secular drift and to give reality to the eternal here in the midst
of time. When it ceases to bear witness to the real presence of an
eternal reality operating in and upon the lives of men, its race is
run; it has missed its mission. But just as certainly the Church
is commissioned as the organ of the Spirit to bring health and
healing to the human lives of men and to the social order in
which these lives are formed and molded.

It may be true, as the realistic higher critics tell us, that the
Kingdom of God as presented in the Gospels is not a new social

order to be slowly, painfully, and creatively realized here in the furrows of our world through the cooperation of God and man together. On the other hand, there is most assuredly a type of life presented in the Gospels which, when it appears, seems to be already the Kingdom of God — a type of life in which love is the supreme spring and motive, in which the spirit of forgiveness has come to ripeness, and which aims to do the will of God on earth as it is done in heaven. In so far as the Church carries on and incarnates that commission it becomes the sower of the seeds of the Kingdom of God and the bearer of a new order for human society.

There is a proverb which says that God empties the nest not by breaking the eggs, but by hatching them. Not by the violent method of revolution will the new social order of life come, not by the legal enforcement of ancient commands, or by the formal application of texts and sayings, but by the vital infusion of a new spirit, the propagation of a passion of love like Christ's, the continuation through the Church of the real presence of Eternity in the midst of time, will something come more like the order of life which we love to call the Kingdom of God. It is the role of the Church, I maintain, to be the fellow laborer with God for this harvest of life. The true Church will be proved to be the true Church, not by its legalistic conformity to the laws and practices of the first century, but by its spirit of love and service, its vision and insight of eternal realities, and its transmissions of the Mind, the Spirit, and the Will of Christ in the world of men.   — Church 110–12, 116–18

BY LITTLE AND BY LITTLE

We no longer expect a world of perfect conditions to appear by sudden intervention. We have explained so many things by the discovery of antecedent developmental processes that we have leaped to the working faith that all things come that way. We do, no doubt, find unbridged gaps in the enormous series of events that have culminated in our present world, and we must admit that nature seems sometimes to desert her usual placid way of process for what looks like a steeple-chase of sudden jumps, but we feel pretty sure that even these jumps have been slowly prepared for and are themselves part of the process-method.

Then, too, we find it very difficult to conceive how a spiritual kingdom — a world which is built and held together by the inner gravitation of love — could come by a fiat, or a stroke, or a jet. The qualities which form and characterize the kingdom of God are all qualities that are born and cultivated within by personal choices, by the formation of rightly-fashioned wills, by the growth of love and sympathy in the heart, by the creation of pure and elevated desires. Those traits must be won and achieved. They cannot be shot into souls from without. If, therefore, we are to expect the crowning age that shall usher in a world in which wrath and hate no longer destroy, from which injustice is banished and the central law of which is love like that of Christ's, then we must look for this age, it seems to me, to come by slow increments and gains of advancing personal and social goodness, and by divine and human processes already at work in some degree in the lives of men.

Christ often seems to teach this view. There is a strand in his sayings that certainly implies a kingdom coming by a long process of slow spiritual gains. There is first the seed, then the blade, then the ear, and finally the full corn in the ear. The mustard seed, though so minute and tiny, is a type of the kingdom because it contains the potentiality of a vast growth and expansion. The yeast is likewise a figure of ever-growing, permeating, penetrating living force which in time leavens the whole mass.

The kingdom is frequently described as an inner life, a victorious spirit. It "comes" when God's will is done in a person as it is done in heaven, and, therefore, it is not a spectacle to be "observed," like the passing of Caesar's legions, or the installation of a new ruler.

But, on the other hand, there are plainly many sayings which point toward the expectation of a mighty sudden event. We seem, again and again, to be hearing not of process, but of apocalypse, not of slow development, but of a mysterious leap. There can be no question that most devout Jews of the first century expected the world's relief expedition to come by miracle, and it is evident that there was an intense hope in the minds of men that, in one way or another, God would intervene and put things right. Many think that Christ shared that hope and expectation.

It is of course possible that in sharing, as He did, the actual life of man, He partook of the hopes and travails and expectations of His times. But, I think, we need to go very slowly and cautiously in this direction. To interpret Christ's message mainly in terms of apocalypse and sudden interventions is surely to miss its naturalness, its spiritual vision, and its inward depth. We can well admit that nobody then had quite our modern conception of process or our present day dislike of breaks, interruptions, and interventions. There was no difficulty in thinking of a new age or dispensation miraculously inaugurated. Only it looks as though Christ had discovered an ethical and spiritual way which made it unnecessary to count on miracles. There was much refuse to be consumed, much corruption to be removed, before the new condition of life could be in full play, but He seems to have seen that the consuming fire and the cleansing work were an essential and inherent part of the *process* that was bringing the kingdom.

When he was asked where men were to look for the king-

dom, His answer was that they were to find a figure and parable
of it in the normal process of nature's scavengers. The carcass
lies decaying in the sun, corrupting the air and tainting everything in its region. There can be no wholesome conditions of
life in that spot until the corruption is removed. But nature has
provided a way of cleansing the air. The scavenger comes and
removes the refuse and corruption and turns it by a strange
alchemy into living matter. Life feeds on the decaying refuse,
raises it back into life, and cleanses the world by making even
corruption minister to its own life processes. We could not live
an hour in our world if it were not alive with a myriad vari-
ety of scavenging methods that burn up effete matter, transmute
noxious forms into wholesome stuff, cleanse away the poisons,
and transmute, not by an apocalypse, but by a process, death
into life and corruption into sweetness. May not the vulture,
like the tiny sparrows who cannot fall without divine regard,
be a sign, a figure, a parable? When we look for the kingdom,
in the light of this sign, we shall not consult the "number of
the beast" — we shall look for it wherever we see life conquering death, wherever the white tents of love are pitched against
the black tents of hate, wherever the living forces of goodness
are battering down the strongholds of evil, wherever the sin-
ner is being changed to a saint, wherever ancient survivals of
instinct and custom are yielding to the sway of growing vision
and insight and ideal.

It is slow and late to come, this kingdom! So was life slow
to come,...so was man slow to come, while fantastic creatures
were tearing each other in the slime. So was a spirit-governed
Person slow to come, while men lived in lust and war and hate.
But in God's world at length the things that ought to come do
come, and we may faintly guess by what we see that the kingdom, too, is coming. There is something like it now in some
lives.   —IL 50–56

LIVING TO LIVE

Christ calls men to a way of life that is *living to live*. It is easy to misinterpret that phrase and to take it with a weak and egoistic meaning. I mean by it first of all a way of life which is cumulative and leads on into ever expanding life, ever new dimensions of life, instead of leading the individual to stop satisfied with secondary, more or less illusory, rewards, which easily come to be themselves ends. But it means a great deal more than that, and we can discover what it really and fully means only when we take pains to see what *life*, in the thought of Christ, opens out into as it spiritually expands, evolves and develops. It begins like the infinitesimal germ of a mustard seed or a yeast spore, but it has the capacity in it of becoming like God, and there appears to be no adequate goal for a spiritual being like us short of that amazing fulfillment of life. There is, however, no possibility of spiritual development toward any stage of perfection along the lonely track of egoism. To live so as to protect and preserve and maintain the rights and privileges of a solitary individual self is to put the poor thin self into peril and to expose it to mortal danger.

We no doubt once used to think of God as bent upon His own honor and glory, and as absorbed in His divine and perfect self — too holy to have any fellowship with sinful men on this low footstool of earth. But that view of God has gone, that is, it has gone for those who know Christ. It could not live a moment in the light of Christ's revelation. Here in that revelation He is a God of grace whose supreme glory is the giving of self in love and tenderness for just such impotent beings as we sinful men are. The conception of Him as an exalted sovereign, always jealous of His dignity and honor, has no place in Christ's thought. Christ's God is not a sovereign; He appears rather as a loving Father whose very inherent nature and character carry

Him into suffering over the sins, defects, and blunders of His children, make Him ready and eager to sacrifice for their sake, and bring Him into the closest inter-relationship and love with beings like us who can be made fully spiritual only by such divine giving and sharing and loving. And thus "to be like God" is to be living a way of life that kills selfishness, obliterates egoism and carries one who seriously intends to live "this way" into self-forgetting and sacrificial deeds of action, though "sacrifice" is not quite the right word to describe deeds done joyously out of sheer love and devotion according to the law and method of the spiritual way of life. The law of the spirit of life in Christ Jesus is a way of radiance and loyalty which expresses His life more truly than the harsh word "sacrifice" does.

We can see best, I think, what this kind of life means when we see how it normally and naturally emerges as a kingdom of God and not as a solitary undertaking. All of the greatest teachers of life have insisted that the personal life must find itself and fulfill itself in a larger group. Plato's *Republic* is the classical attempt to tell how the microcosm, which the individual is, must be seen and studied in the macrocosm of a social whole. Aristotle in the same way sees every ethical trait and virtue of "the good man" revealed in and through relationships with others. He considers one man alone as no man at all. This social group idea has become as essential to our present-day theories of ethical goodness as gravitation is to physics. It is, too, indissolubly bound up with the meaning and fulfillment of the Galilean way of life.

Living to live is living as an organic part of a kingdom, a fellowship, which expresses in visible and temporal fashion, in ever-growing and unfolding degrees, the will of God — the heart and purpose and spirit of the divine life. Here in this kingdom God's life differentiates itself and pours itself through finite lives as the sap of the vine pours itself out into all the branches and twigs and shoots which go together to make the vine a vine. It is the vast Ygdrasil tree of a spiritual humanity. The kingdom, even in its imperfect stage as we now see it — still a good deal of a mustard seed — is the most impressive revelation of God there is in the world today. It is the only way that the will and life and love of God can be fully revealed. In this emergent group-life, where love comes more fully into play than it does anywhere else, we catch some gleams of the Great Life that works through us now and some prophecies of that kingdom which shall be when all men see what a few see now.

Life culminates in forms of organism, in which the whole is always greater than the sum of the parts. The kingdom of God is the highest form of such organism that has yet emerged — a *corpus spirituale*, "a blessed community" — a living whole in which part contributes to part, and all the parts unitedly co-operate to express the life of the whole. Each member is both end and means, an end in itself and a means to the fulfillment of the life and purpose of the whole. We are as far removed here as we can be from a scheme of life which focuses upon rewards or which aims to secure an excess of pleasures over pains. In fact we have transcended categories of calculation and even of causation and have entered into that organic way of life, where each lives for all and where the interpretation of the Life of the Whole is the business and at the same time the joy of each unit-member. The formation of such a kingdom, life in such a kingdom, is the fundamental end of life for Christ, as set forth in the Gospels. The length of His purpose horizontally is the inclusion of all men in such a cooperative brotherhood and the height of it upward is the raising of all men to a full consciousness of sonship with God, in a family-fellowship, living to do His will. Here, once more, the emphasis of Christ is on life and action, not on theory and definition. The kingdom of God is something men *do* — not a place to which they go.

The model prayer asks for the kingdom of God to come and instantly explains it by adding, "thy will be *done* on earth." That *is* the kingdom, and we are in it when we are allied with God in making His will come to deed throughout the earth, or here in our little fraction of it....

Man is forever seeking to find the whole of himself, but his sporadic quests lead him off on trails that end in some cul-de-sac, or, as Emerson would say, "up a tree in a squirrel hole." His subordinate ends bring and have always brought frustration, disillusionment, and defeat. Let him once find the real end for which his nature is equipped and he can live thrillingly and triumphantly. That real end, according to the Christ of the Gospels, is the kingdom of God, a spiritual organism, a fellowship of persons, bound together in cooperative love and forming in union with God the tissue and web of the spiritual World — the eternal Universe. To this end were we born and for this cause we came into the world that we might bear witness to this reality and that we might reveal its laws, its principles, and its serene and demonstrative power.   — FE 58–63

THE SECOND MILE

Let us endeavor to recover for our thought that central conquering faith which lay at the heart of primitive Christianity, when it first became apostolic, which literally means "missionary." It was on its highest level a new revelation of God, and it was on the human plane an equally new revelation of man's potential nature. We have not got back to the heart of Christianity until we have recovered both of these essential aspects of Christ's life and message. They are so completely woven together that either one is apt to be missed if the other is overlooked, as has too often happened in the course of Christian history.

Christ leaps, by a supreme spiritual insight, to a wholly new revelation of the essential character of God and consequently of life itself. God is eternally Father. He does not become Father through some mysterious change in his nature, or on account of some transaction that has occurred, nor does he ever cease to have the character traits of Father. Creation is as much an expression of Father-love as redemption is. Love is the one method of soul-making.

The shift of approach from the legal level to that of grace is as momentous a change of level as is the shift from the stage of matter to that of life, or from the vegetable kingdom to that of the animal. Something that would have been unthinkable on the lower level emerges on the higher level. It is as though one should pass from air-waves to radio-vibrations, or from molecular-processes to the inner process of consciousness. The compulsion of a soul is as much a contradiction of terms as the persuasion of a stone wall by argument would be.

Jesus was the interpreter of this way of life to a degree beyond that reached or expressed by anyone who has lived on earth. It must be said further that in the person of Christ we pass beyond what is usually meant by an interpreter of a way of life. His life has seemed to men in all generations to stand forth as a unique and attractive ideal of what life at its best and highest should be. St. Paul called him "a new Adam," a new creation, a new type of humanity. In saying that, St. Paul was thinking of him primarily as the beginning of a new order of life-giving spirit — that is to say, as a typical incarnation of love and self-giving. Jesus expected to see the miracle of transformation through love work on sin-crippled men and women in every walk of life.

This appeal of love called out the potential Cephas hidden and hardly suspected in the impulsive Simon. It raised a sinning woman, whose hope and expectation were gone, to a pure and radiant saint. It changed a self-despised tax collector into an honest and self-respecting man. It was instantly recognized by responsive little children. It had an almost miraculous effect on demoniacs who had been rendered more insane by methods of terror and compulsion.

It seemed to fail in Pilate's Hall and at Golgotha. It did not soften the hate of crafty politicians or touch the quick of Roman soldiers. The jeer of the mob drowned out the gentle voice of forgiving love. To the onlookers the "defeat" seemed obvious. But somehow that Cross has touched the heart of the world as nothing else has ever done, and it has through the ages been the most redemptive power of which history has any record.

From the very first stages of his mission Christ identified this way of grace and self-giving to which he was dedicated with the eternal character of God. His test of any quality of life was always to see whether it made the possessor of it more like God. "You are to love, even your enemies, so that you may be like God; you are to be peacemakers so that you may be recognized as God's children." And the inevitable doom that goes with it is that a soul cannot be forgiven that cannot recognize love and forgiveness when they are bestowed upon it. To lose love is by an inescapable law of life to lose God.

The parables which interpret the heart of God, with utmost naturalness and simplicity, take for granted that love is the essential aspect of his character. Lilies in the field and mother birds brooding on their nests are symbols for him of a divine care existing at the heart of things. The thoughtful gift of a cup of cold water to a little child in need stores up an increment of love in the spiritual world which is never lost or wasted.

The unforgettable parables, which we owe to St. Luke, carry this identity of love with God to its highest possible expression in words. The shepherd seeking his lost sheep, the woman hunting for her lost coin, the father meeting his returning son who had gone wrong — utterly simple stories and yet immortal frescoes of reality — carry the mind of the reader unconsciously and irresistibly from incidents of village life in Palestine to an eternal quality in the heart of God.

The fact that God can be revealed in a personal life carries momentous implications. It means that the Divine and the human are not so far sundered as had been persistently supposed. It means that human nature *can become* an organ for the Life of God since it *has been* such an organ. It means that God is nearer to us than we supposed; more truly an Emmanuel God than we had been wont to believe. It may well be that God is all along endeavoring to break through and reveal his presence and character, the only difficulty being that he finds such poor, self-filled instruments for any true revelation to break through.

This revealing union of the Divine and the human in a life of love and service and self-giving is the clue to another central idea which belongs to the heart of Christianity — namely, the way of life which Christ called "the Kingdom of God." This phrase has had many meanings during the period of Christian history, and, as it stands expressed in the Gospels, it is open to more than a single interpretation. The first century, in which the New Testament came to birth, was an age of apocalyptic expectations; and the despair of getting spiritual results by natural processes, which characterizes all apocalypses, is undoubtedly in evidence throughout the New Testament, as is also the fervid hope that a supernatural relief expedition was near at hand.

But the remarkable fact is that there is another far deeper and more unique strand there of a wholly different type. It is easy to see how the apocalyptic hope got its place in the story; it is not so easy to account for the amazing depth and originality of the central insight which constitutes here the heart of the message, which is the process of the coming of the Life of God into the lives of men.

The great saying, "The Kingdom of God is within you," has been called by a modern Hindu the greatest revelation that any person has ever made. But it is not a solitary saying, apart and alone, and out of keeping with the rest of the sayings. It is rather a key which opens the whole meaning of the unique conception of the Kingdom. And it is the Kingdom which forms the deepest and most original strand of the message of "good news," which we call "Gospel."

The world has suffered serious loss by the constant assumption that the Kingdom of God is a post-mortem state instead of being a positive Christian ideal of life for the individual and for society here in this world where it is so desperately needed. The otherworldly emphasis in Christian teaching has accustomed us to postpone our holy cities and our rivers of the water of life to a realm beyond the grave. We have taken the Kingdom of God as a final gift when we should have thought of it as a present task — the citizenship of the new humanity according to the measure of "the new Adam," its founder.

Whatever else the Kingdom of God may be in its full meaning, it is in its very nature a way of life which must begin first of all within the life of a person. Whatever more it may be, it is at least a kind of society in which the spirit of love and peace that ruled and controlled Christ's life has become the inward law and nature of those who compose it. Christ once, in a striking passage, called the method "going the second mile." He saw how much of life and religion was "legal," how many things were done because they were expected or required or compelled, and when they were performed they were counted up and cashed in for merit. To Him this first mile of compulsion, this carefully measured mile, had almost no significance for real life as it ought to be. When the second-mile spirit is born one is ready to cut off a right hand, or pluck out an eye, for the adventure, for the goal, without stopping to think of the loss.

The world is so accustomed to the methods of secular calculation and rationalization that this other way seems absurd and
forbidding. It has never been tried on a large scale or in a bold,
determined fashion. God's poor little man of Assisi went all the
way through with it as his method, and the world reverently
preserves the scenes of his life as among its most sacred shrines.
But it is one thing to canonize a thirteenth-century saint and
another to take up, adapt, and carry on his adventure in the
twentieth century. John Woolman was a humble second-mile
saint in the eighteenth century, and once more he demonstrated
the conquering power of love and grace — "the lamb made war
against the beast and overcame it." But there is still much more
territory to win. For there can be little question that this spiritual adventure with the quiet force of love and cooperative good
will lies at the very heart of the Gospel of Christ, and is the
main business of Christ's men in the world.   — SP 192–201

4

Building the Kingdom

Jones has already told us that God's Kingdom is "held together by the inner gravitation of love," and that Christ, "the divine love existing at the heart of things," calls each of us to co-operate actively in its building. The kingdom is something we do, not somewhere we go. In the following selections, he re-flects on several ways we mature in the Body of Christ and work towards the coming of the Kingdom. The inspiration for these strategies comes in large part from Jones's Quaker back-ground. But their wisdom crosses sectarian borders to strike at the heart of what it means to be a committed Christian living in the world.

Prayer, that most "extraordinary" and "astonishing" of acts, is one way in which the Kingdom is built. In its essence, prayer is immediate spiritual fellowship, uniting the prayerful heart with both the Beyond within and with fellow humans. Simplicity in life and religion, as well as a deep-seated commitment to ideals such as peace and economic justice, are others. Tolerance for all faith-traditions, which allows for organic unity among believers and repudiates soul-killing institutionalism, is also an essential strategy. All of these attitudes and actions ultimately contribute to a new world held together by the spiritual gravitation of love,

*a world where there is no longer a divide between the secular and
the profane, a world in which God indeed is Emmanuel.*

PRAYER

Prayer is an extraordinary act. The eyes close, the face lights up,
the body is moved with feeling, and (it may be in the presence
of a multitude) the person praying talks in perfect confidence
with somebody, invisible and intangible, and who articulates no
single word of response. It is astonishing. And yet it is a human
custom as old as marriage, as ancient as grave-making, older
than any city on the globe. There is no human activity which
so stubbornly resists being reduced to a bread-and-butter basis.
Men have tried to explain the origin of prayer by the straits of
physical hunger, but it will no more fit into utilitarian systems
than joy over beauty will. It is an elemental and unique attitude
of the soul and it will not be explained until we fathom the
origin of the soul itself.

But is not the advance of science making prayer impossible?
In unscientific ages the universe presented no rigid order. It was
easy to believe that the ordinary course of material processes
might be altered or reversed. The world was conceived as full
of invisible beings who could affect the course of events at will,
while above all, there was a Being who might interfere with
things at any moment, in any way.

Our world today is not so conceived. Our universe is organized and linked. Every event is caused. Caprice is banished.
There is no such thing in the physical world as an uncaused
event.... Even the weather is no more capricious than the
course of a planet in space. Every change of wind and the
course of every flying cloud is determined by previous conditions. Complex these combinations of circumstances are, but if

the weather man could get data enough he could foretell the storm, the rain, the drought, exactly as well as the astronomer can foretell the eclipse. There is no little demon, there is no tall, bright angel, who holds back the shower or who pushes the cloud before him; no being, good or bad, who will capriciously alter the march of molecules because it suits our fancy to ask that the chain of causes be interrupted. What is true of the weather is true in every physical realm. Our universe has no caprice in it....

The knowledge of this iron situation has had a desolating effect upon many minds. The heavens have become as brass and the earth bars of iron. To ask for the interruption of the march of atoms seems to the scientific thinker the absurdest of delusions and all fanes of prayer appear fruitless. Others resort to the faith that there are gaps in the causal system and that in these unorganized regions — the domains so far unexplored — these are realms for miracle and divine wonder. The supernatural, on this theory, is to be found out beyond the region of the natural, and forcing itself through the gaps. Those of this faith are filled with dread as they see the so-called gaps closing, somewhat as the pious Greek dreaded to see Olympus climbed.

There are still others who evade the difficulty by holding that God has made the universe, is the Author of its laws, is Omnipotent and therefore can change them at will, or can admit exceptions in their operation.... This view takes us back once more into a world of caprice. It introduces a world in which almost anything may happen. We can no longer calculate upon anything with assurance.... But this is not all: it is a low, crude view of God — a Being off above the world who makes laws like a modern legislator and again changes them to meet a new situation, who is after all only a bigger man in the sky busily moving and shifting the scenes of the time-drama as requests reach him.

None of these positions is tenable. The first is not, for prayer is a necessity to full life, and the other two are not, because they do not fairly face the facts which are forced upon those who accept scientific methods of search and of thought. This physical universe is a stubborn affair. It is not loose and adjustable, and worked, for our private convenience, by wires or strings at a central station....

The real difficulty is that our generation has been conceiving of prayer on too low a plane. Faith is not endangered by the advance of science. It is endangered by the stagnation of religious conceptions. If religion halts at some primitive level and science marches on to new conquests of course there will be difficulty. But let us not fetter science, let us rather promote religion. We need to rise to a truer view of God and to a loftier idea of prayer....

The prayer which science *has* affected is the spurious kind of prayer, which can be reduced to a utilitarian, bread-and-butter basis. Most enlightened persons now are shocked to hear "patriotic" ministers asking God to direct the bullets of their country's arm so as to kill their enemies in battle, and we all hesitate to use prayer for the attainment of low, selfish ends, but we need to cleanse our sight still farther and rise above the conceptions of prayer as an easy means to a desired end....

We have not to do with a God who is "off there" above the sky, who can deal with us only through the violation of physical law. We have instead a God "in whom we live and move and are," whose Being opens into ours, and ours into His, who is the very Life of our lives, the matrix of our personality; and there is no separation between us unless we make it ourselves. No man, scientist or layman, knows where the curve is to be drawn about the personal "self." No man can say with authority that the circulation of divine currents into the soul's inward life is impossible. On the contrary, Energy does come in. In the highest moments we find ourselves in contact with wider spiritual Life than belongs to our normal "me."

But true prayer is something higher. It is immediate spiritual fellowship. Even if science could demonstrate that prayer could never effect any kind of utilitarian results, still prayer on its loftier side would remain untouched, and persons of spiritual reach would go on praying as before. If we could say nothing more we could at least affirm that prayer, like faith, is itself the victory. The seeking is the finding. The wrestling is the blessing. It is no more a means to something else than love is. It is an end in itself. It is its own excuse for being. It is a kind of first fruit of the mystical nature of personality. The edge of the self is always touching a circle of life beyond itself to which it responds. The human heart is sensitive to God as the retina is to light waves. The soul possesses a native yearning for intercourse and companionship which takes it to God as naturally as the home instinct of the pigeon takes it to the place of its birth. There is in every normal soul a spontaneous outreach, a free play of spirit which gives it onward yearning of unstilled desire.

It is no mere subjective instinct — no blind outreach. If it met no response, no answer, it would soon be weeded out of the race. It would shrivel like the functionless organ. We could not long continue to pray in faith if we lost the assurance that there is a Person who cares, and who actually corresponds with us. Prayer has stood the test of experience. In fact the very desire to pray is in itself prophetic of a heavenly Friend. A subjective need always carries an implication of an objective stimulus which has provoked the need. There is no hunger for anything not tasted, there is no search for anything which is not in the environment, for the environment has always produced the appetite. So this native need of the soul rose out of the divine origin of the soul, and it has steadily verified itself as a safe guide to reality.

What is at first a vague life-activity and spontaneous outreach of inward energy — a feeling after companionship — remains in many persons vague to the end. But in others it frequently rises to a definite consciousness of a personal Presence and there comes back into the soul a compelling evidence of a real Other Self who meets all the Soul's needs. For such persons prayer is the way to fullness of life. It is as natural as breathing. It is as normal an operation as appreciation of beauty, or the pursuit of truth. The soul is made that way, and as long as men are made with mystical deeps within, unsatisfied with the finite and incomplete, they will pray and be refreshed.

Vague and formless, in some degree, communion would always be, I think, apart from the personal manifestation of God in Jesus Christ. As soon as God is known as Father, as soon as we turn to Him as identical in being with our own humanity, as suffering with us and loving us even in our imperfection, this communion grows defined and becomes actual social fellowship which is prayer at its best. Paul's great prayers of fellowship rise to the God and Father of our Lord Jesus Christ, the God whom we know, because He has been humanly revealed in a way that fits our life. We turn to Him as the completeness and reality of all we want to be, the other Self whom we have always sought. The vague impulse to reach beyond our isolated and solitary self gives place to an actual experience of relationship with a personal Friend and Companion and this experience may become, and often does become, the loftiest and most joyous activity of life. The soul is never at its best until it enjoys God, and prays out of sheer love. Nobody who has learned to pray in this deeper way and whose prayer is a prayer of communion and fellowship, wants logical argument for the existence of a God. Such a want implies a fall from a higher to a lower level. It is like a demand for a proof of the beauty one feels, or an evidence of love other than the evidence of its experience.

Prayer will always rise or fall with the quality of one's faith, like the mercury in the tube which feels at once the change of pressure in the atmosphere. It is only out of live faith that a living prayer springs. When a man's praying sinks into words, words, words, it means that he is trying to get along with a dead conception of God. The circuit no longer closes. He cannot heighten his prayer by raising his voice. What he needs is a new revelation of the reality of God. He needs to have the fresh sap of living faith in God to push off the dead leaves of an outgrown belief, so that once more prayer shall break forth as naturally as buds in spring.

The conception of God as a lonely Sovereign, complete in Himself and infinitely separated from us grasshoppers chirping our brief hour in the sun, is in the main a dead notion. Prayer to such a God would not be easy with our modern ideas of the universe. But that whole conception is being supplanted by a live faith in an Infinite Person who is corporate with our lives, from whom we have sprung, in whom we live, as far as we spiritually do live, who needs us as we need him, and who is sharing with us the travail and the tragedy as well as the glory and the joy of bringing forth sons of God.

In such a kingdom — an organic fellowship of interrelated persons — prayer is as normal an activity as gravitation is in a world of matter. Personal spirits experience spiritual gravitation, soul reaches after soul, hearts draw toward each other. We are no longer in the net of blind fate, in the realm of impersonal force, we are in a love-system where the aspiration of one member heightens the entire group, and the need of one — even the least — draws upon the resources of the whole — even the Infinite. We are in actual divine-human fellowship.

The only obstacle to effectual praying, in this world of spiritual fellowship, would be individual selfishness. To want to get just for one's own self, to ask for something which brings loss and injury to others, would be to sever one's self from the source of blessings, and to lose not only the thing sought but to lose, as well, one's very self.

This principle is true anywhere, even in ordinary human friendship. It is true, too, in art and in music. The artist may not force some personal caprice into his creation. He must make himself the organ of a universal reality which is beautiful not simply for this man or that, but for man as man. If there is, as I believe, an inner kingdom of spirit, a kingdom of love and fellowship, then it is a fact that a tiny being like one of us can impress and influence the Divine Heart, and we can make our personal contribution to the Will of the universe, but we can do it only by wanting what everybody can share and by seeking blessings which have a universal implication.

So far as prayer is real fellowship, it gives as well as receives. The person who wants to receive God must first bring himself. If he misses us, we miss Him. He is in Spirit, and consequently He is found only through true and genuine spiritual activity. In this correspondence of fellowship there is no more violation of natural law than there is in love wherever it appears. Love is itself the principle of the spiritual universe, as gravitation is of the physical; and as in the gravitate system the earth rises to meet the ball of the child, without breaking any law, so God comes to meet and to heighten the life of anyone who stretches up toward Him in appreciation, and there is joy above as well as below. —DS 89–111

THE SIMPLE LIFE

No one of us ever knows quite what he wants. Ask almost any young man what he wants to become and he will answer, "I don't know yet." He is waiting for somebody, or some occasion to help him discover himself, to reveal to him what his own life

means to him. Strange paradox, that I do not know even what
I myself want, and that I need outside help to discover the ideal
of my own life. Such, however, is the actual fact, as every one of
us who has groped and striven for his life's goal can testify. But
if a self-conscious person seldom knows fully and clearly what
he is aiming to realize, much less does a group, or a society, or a
nation know its own purpose and aim. The guides and prophets
of a people are the men or the women who catch glimpses of
the true line of march, and so can reveal to the group, large or
small, what it wants and how it can fulfill its own destiny.

It is often astonishing to see the power of a phrase which
some man coined — a magic word which goes from tongue to
tongue, as though a new Pentecost were abroad. It is astonishing until we realize that this man, by a stroke of genius, has
hit the word which expresses what everybody is more or less
blindly feeling after. He has become a voice, not crying in the
wilderness, but a voice uttering the need and purpose of his generation, and if the time is ripe enough and the word is dynamic
enough, a reformation, or a revival, or a renascence will follow.
"The Simple Life" is one of these magic words because it comes
to a world weary and heavy laden with its gigantic tasks and its
enormous complexities — it comes as a revelation of what we
all know we want, as soon as somebody has the genius to discover it for us! So far, however, the simple life is hardly more
than a happy phrase. We know we want it, but we have not
quite discovered what it is....

Simplicity is first of all a *quality of the soul,* and we must see
what it means within, in the spirit....

The first Christians "ate their bread with gladness and singleness (or, as we should say, simplicity) of heart." One of our
Master's deepest words was, "If your eye be single (i.e., simple)
your whole body will be full of light." Now what does that
mean? It is just the opposite of duplicity or doubleness. Our

best modern word for it is perhaps "sincerity," absence of every tinge and tone of sham. For the Quaker, "the simple life" has always begun there. There can be no genuine simplicity in the relationships of life, if there is not unclouded honesty at the heart and center.

Oliver Wendell Holmes has somewhere described minute forms of life so transparent that one can look through their bodies and see the lungs breathe and the heart beat. Such transparency of purpose, such purity of intention and motive is the very basis of any simple life which is to refresh and recreate our modern society. The first demand is for persons whose souls are as untainted with duplicity and sham as the air of the arctic zone is untainted with the germs of disease.

"The simple life," we shall say, then, begins when a person is found who is absolutely honest with himself, who will not have either the world or God think him to be what he is not in his own soul, who will have no victories if they cannot be won without bartering the priceless jewel of his own sincerity. . . .

One has often heard that the simplest things are the most difficult. It is easier to write a history of civilization than it is to describe consciousness, and it is doubtless easier to be Prime Minister of England than to be a "simple" person such as I have indicated. It is an ideal for us all rather than an attainment, but it is worth emphasizing that we can never hope for the simple life in the great world of society until we have persons who begin their honesty by being honest with themselves in the dark, persons who can say with the brave old psalmist, "Thou hast visited me in the night and found nothing," i.e., nothing false or crooked.

But most of our life, whether it is simple or complex, is a life of relationships with other persons. It is this fact of interrelationships that makes life spiritual, and it is this that often makes it so tragic. We cannot, if we would, fence round our souls and keep them naked and alone. We are good and bad, not in soul-tight compartments, but in our dealings with other persons who fill our world.

Our highest dealings, those which affect our entire being in the profoundest way, are our relationships with God. Nothing else so completely shapes one's whole nature as his way of responding to his Infinite Companion, for everybody does respond in one way or another. Perhaps in no other field of human activity is the doctrine of the simple life so much needed as in religion. Few earthly things are more complicated than the theology of the creeds and the schools. It is dry, abstract, involved and logical. The shades of difference between this group and that group are so subtle and finely drawn that only the experts can distinguish them. The ordinary man with an immortal soul in him looks upon all this load of theology as a very expensive luxury. It does not touch his daily life and it possesses little living interest or value for him. Consequently much of the preaching in the churches moves in a realm foreign to the modern man of busy life; it does not feed his soul. His problems are all practical and concrete, and he has no ear for abstract sermons, i.e., sermons which deal with wordy distinctions. The service, too, strikes many of our practical citizens, with their lives crowded full of work and business, as being artificial and devoid of significance. This again is too complicated and too much of a luxury for their simple tastes. It does not rest them; it rather wearies them. The mass of men today who seem nonreligious or irreligious are often not so in fact. They do not find their needs met. They want a simple religion and they do not find it.

Has Quakerism anything to tell the world about simplicity in religion? It has. This is the main secret of its remarkable success in its early days. It was as simple as the Galilean's Gospel. It made no compromise with an interminable mass of scholastic theology. It cut loose from it all. One sentence from George Fox announces its whole program — "Let nothing come between your souls and God but Jesus Christ." There was a proclamation of large principles, but no creed. Quakerism was a religion of simple trust and confidence in a divine Father, and a life of willing obedience to His will revealed directly to the soul. Those who came flocking to the new Society were not asked what they believed about abstract doctrine, but simply if they were ready to obey the Light. There was no technical service. They tried to make everything which furthered life sacramental. The religious meeting was modeled after the family life. Those who composed it came together with no officials, in a technical sense, no professional leaders, no set program, no artificial contrivances. They sat down together as children of a common Father, and let the Spirit direct the exercises freely and spontaneously. There were times when the tides of life ran high, and the attenders went home refreshed as though they had drunk from the cup of the Holy Grail. It was a religion of the simple life. There was no heavy load of superstitions to warp the true bent of the soul, but each person was called to stand on his own feet for free and open intercourse with God.

You will look in vain through all the early books for any exact definition even of the "inner Light." Nobody tried to define it in abstract words. Every sentence about it is an appeal to the persons addressed to find out what it is by a stainless purity of heart, and by an implicit obedience to "that of God" in themselves. There is to be nothing thrust in which shall prevent any person from having his own intimate fellowship with God in ways which fit his own deep human needs. The beginning, end and middle of true Quaker teaching is that simple word at Jacob's well: "God is spirit, and they that worship Him must do it in spirit and in truth," or genuineness.

Few things are more needed today than this plain, simple note, that religion on its upward reaching side is just joyous companionship with God — with God who is nearer than Abraham realized when he talked with Him at his tent door, or Jacob dreamed when he saw Heaven at the far end of a ladder.

But I must hasten on to point out the practical and social character of Quaker simplicity. The Quaker fronted a world full of artificial complexity, a society of classes, amounting almost to castes. He met it with the simple, single idea that every man, high or low, ignorant or learned, rich or poor, white or colored, good or bad, was to be treated as a potential child of God, and so a brother.... So long as men use other men solely for their own ends, whether it be at the polls, or in the shop, or in the saloon, there will remain some form of slavery. It is the very essence of tyranny to treat a person as though he were a thing, to use him as a tool.

The Quaker panacea for the ills of boss-ridden states, for the warfare between labor and capital, for the inhumanity of the saloon and the white slave traffic is the simple method of propagating a genuine brotherhood. Treat every person as a brother.

The supreme weakness of the Church has been its tendency to withdraw from the actual problems of this present world, to construct an abstract theory of goodness, and to consider religion too sacred a thing to be risked in the rough and tumble of daily contact with this woefully imperfect world. Brotherhood has been narrowed to brotherhood among saints. Humanity has been split into two groups — the Church and the world. The gap is artificial. To the true Quaker, every person the heavenly Father has made is a brother. If he has the scars and brands of evil upon him, if he has been bestead and wounded by the archers, all the more he needs the medicine of love and the balm of a brother's tender sympathy. Religion of simplicity creates no lines of division. It builds no compartments. Rather it wipes out such artificial barriers. Men are men, and they are to be treated as brothers to the last. It is this spirit which has reformed prisons, fought slavery, championed the cause of the Indian and freedman, striven to alleviate suffering everywhere, and quietly wrought in city and country to make peace supplant war, and love hatred. Again, we must admit, and realize that the path of simplicity is a slow and difficult one. If our social goal is a kingdom of brothers we need not look for that millennium by express tomorrow. It is a far, far remote consummation. Few of us even yet actually practice it ourselves, but it is nevertheless the only path, even though over Alps, to a renewed and regenerated world, and the pillar Friends of all epochs have walked it and have called us into it....

We come now to the world-old problem of how to live a Christian life, not in a cloister or an anchorite's cave, but in an eager, busy, complex world of more or less imperfect men and women. The saint of an earlier day tried to cut the knot by withdrawal. He climbed a lonely pillar, or he buried himself in a quiet cell, but even so he could not escape the self which he carried with him. All his problems came back in new fashion, and as far as he succeeded in cutting the bonds which bound him to his fellows he found himself shrinking and shriveling like a severed branch.

The endeavor to win goodness by withdrawal from society is as vain as the search for the lost fountain or the pursuit of an alchemy which will make gold out of lead. The only possible way to overcome the world is to carry the forces of the spiritual life into the veins of society until peace and love and righteousness prevail there.

We can best discover the principle of the simple life by a contrast with the spirit of commercialism. The commercial spirit is selfish. Its motto is "Expand to get." Even its philanthropies are selfish. They are to whitewash gigantic schemes of absorption. Its culture is selfish. It is veneer and display. The trail of selfishness is on its art and music and religion and recreation.... It is the old pagan Roman spirit modernized and sprinkled with a little baptismal water, but essentially the spirit of selfishness — the pursuit of power, pleasure, and luxury for their own sake. Over against it, at its antipodes, is the spirit of the simple life. It can be lived at any level of poverty or wealth; and at any stage of ignorance or culture. It is essentially the spirit of living for life's sake, or consecration to personal and social goodness. Its first aim is making a life rather than making a living. This spirit does not keep a man out of commercial business, nor does it command him to confine his business to narrow limits and to small returns. But if he is to belong to the goodly fellowship of those who live the simple life, his business must be made an avenue of ministering to human life. It must be to him what the mission field is to the missionary — a sphere for manifesting his consecration to service. "If I were not a priest," says Tauler, an apostle of the simple life in the fourteenth century, "I should esteem it a gift of the Holy Ghost that I was able to make shoes." And we may add that the latter occupation may be turned to divine service as well as the other....

The same principle applies to culture. There are no limits to the pursuit of culture so long as it is sought in the spirit of consecration and for ends of service. Like the Master, who fully embodied the idea of the simple life, we can say, "For their sakes I enlarge and cultivate myself, that others may also enter a more abundant life." The test of any of the culture-fields is whether it can be made a means of personal enlargement and of wider consecration. Poetry, art, and music belong to the simple life, if they minister to man's larger life, and they do not belong there if they do not so minister. The question is not one of theory, but one of practice. Beauty is as genuine a reality as truth is, and so is harmony. Pursued in the aim of enlargement and for widening the area of life and happiness they are as legitimate and as "simple" as the reading of *Pilgrim's Progress* or *Piety Promoted*. Doubtless they may be turned to low ends, but so, too, may all other earthly pursuits. The easy solution is to hedge life about with "thou shalt nots," to draw a narrow circle and to limit life to beaten paths of commonplace virtue. But that produces mediocre lives. It squeezes life down to a level of sameness. It endangers advance and risks the extinction of originality, freshness, and power. Simplicity is not barrenness. It is singleness of aim and purpose....

The principle has, in most perfect words, been expressed by John Woolman: "To turn all we possess into the channel of universal love becomes the business of our lives." That is the Quaker message about the simple life. The pillar Friends have always preached enlargement of life, but they have, at the same time, guarded the simplicity of life by pulsing a single purpose through all their pursuits, and by baptizing their culture with the dew of consecration. On this principle there are no dangers. The full life may be as simple as the barren life, the life which brings in spoil from every field of culture may possess the simple directness of a line of light.   — QS 7–33

UNITY, NOT UNIFORMITY

The divisions in the Church itself and its failure to confront its tasks with vision and leadership and creative power constitute, if the truth were frankly uttered, the supreme difficulty which confronts the Christian interpretation of life in the world today. Organization in a subtle, more or less unconscious way tends to become an end in itself and may even defeat the very ideals and aims it exists to promote and foster. The power and authority of a great system, made august and sacred by time and perspective, fit rather badly with the spiritual demands of personal freedom, initiative and fresh creative leadership. Ecclesiasticism does not easily keep house on friendly terms with a growing faith of first-hand experience and inward vision. The natural conservatism of a great historic religious body is bound to produce a dampening effect on glowing and original minds, and it makes it difficult for the prophets of a new age, when they appear, to find scope for their transforming work. The importance of the preservation of the inheritance from the past cultivates an attitude of caution and inclines an ancient organization to defend the status quo, to stand sponsor for outgrown customs, and to protect forms of worship and systems of thought which have become inadequate for the expanding life of the race. We are only too familiar with the tendency to compromise, the lack of social vision, the failure to see, as from a mountain top, the dawn of new epochs and to give prophetic leadership in times of moral crisis....

There has been a curious and yet widespread tendency manifested to confuse unity with uniformity. They are totally different. The former is of the highest importance; in fact, it is an essential feature of a Church that is to be effectual. Uniformity, on the other hand, is disastrous, even deadly. It levels down instead of up. It cramps and compels the mind. It is mechanistic and not spiritual. It is even conceivable that a tightly organized and uniform Church, which allowed no freedom of deviation, might present more dangers and difficulties to the spread of Christ's Christianity than are to be found in the divided Church of the present.

A few years ago, someone, in friendly conversation with one of the leading American officials of the Roman Catholic Church, asked him what he would say if he saw a person who obviously possessed and manifested grace in his life and yet never made use of what his Church called "the means of grace," or "the channels of grace." Without a moment's hesitation, the distinguished Churchman replied: "I should say that he belonged to the invisible Church and I should say further that it is more important to belong to the invisible Church than to the visible one."

No one could question the breadth or the liberality of that answer. It is exactly the position that was taken in the sixteenth century by a number of profound spiritual prophets [Anabaptists] who regretted to see the reformers of that epoch laboring to set up another infallible visible Church to take the place of the one against which they were protesting. These spiritual prophets were afraid of organizations and forms and systems. They hoped to have the spirit of love and truth and gentleness propagated through personal lives and they believed that the Light and Life of Christ as Eternal Spirit could be forever born anew in the hearts of saints without the necessity for any visible body anywhere in the world to be the incarnation of it.

This is a very popular and a taking theory in the world today. It avoids the dangers of a great organization. It entails no burdens. It imposes no statement of creed. It loads no inherited cargo of ideas upon the tender backs of an unborn generation. It trusts to the contagious power of truth and love. The ideal is, no doubt, a beautiful one which has attracted and fascinated many noble souls at many different periods of human history. But it is almost certainly a dream rather than a solid reality. There might, no doubt, be a world in which truth and love are transmitted and propagated by invisible contagions without any visible organ of preservation and transmission, but it seems pretty certain that we are not living in that kind of a world. The spiritual, as we know it, is never disembodied, existing apart by itself in isolation and floating intangibly above the realm which we inhabit. The spiritual is conjunct with the physical. The one is superposed on the other. However unlike they may be, they belong together and both suffer by division into sundered halves.

In spite of these dangers, therefore, which beset organizations, institutions, and systems, and in spite of their tendency
to smother the truth they carry, there appears to be no solution of the problem of the transmission of the Life and Love
and Truth of God revealed in Christ without the existence of
a visible corporate body in the world as the organ of its apprehension and transmission. The most urgent problem before
us today, if we are eager to carry spiritual vision and power
into the life of our present day world, is the task of drawing
the branches of the Christian Church together into one living
whole, sufficiently unified to be an organ of the Spirit, and possessed of wisdom and power enough to attract into its wide
family life the multitude of spiritually minded persons who at
present have no religious home and no group fellowship.

The best type of organization for the preservation and transmission of the precious spiritual treasure which constitutes the
heart of Christianity would seem to be one that approached as
closely as possible to a living, growing *organism,* and that was
as far removed as possible from a *mechanism,* though organizations tend by their law of habit and custom to slide in the
mechanistic direction. St. Paul is one of the greatest interpreters
of the organic type of Church that ever lived. Again and again
he used the human body with its vital functions as his best il-
lustrations of the unique organism that was to be Christ's new
Body in the world. "You are the Body of Christ," he solemnly
reminds his Corinthian believers, "and each one of you is a
particular member of it" (1 Cor. 12:27). And he proceeds to
explain how this living Body which was to be the reincarnation
of Christ was to be led, guided, directed, and taught by persons
endowed with spiritual "gifts" rather than by technical officials
(1 Cor. 12:28–34). That there might be no doubt in anyone's
mind what was in his thought, the highest gift and qualifica-
tion for spiritual leadership, he gave the immortal description

of the gift in the Hymn of Love in the thirteenth chapter of First Corinthians. The spirit of love which suffers long and is kind towers over all other qualifications and far surpasses that knowledge of speculation which puffs up the possessor with pride and sets one group of speculators against another group with a different set of speculative ideas and ends, sooner or later, in division if not in hate and hostility. Love, for St. Paul, is the heart of the organic type of Church.

In a flash of insight, while he was living in Ephesus, where he daily saw the famous Temple of Diana, he leaped to the novel idea that a person could be a temple. "Know you not that you are temples?" he wrote to the members of the Corinthian Church. Gradually the idea ripened and expanded, and when he wrote his Epistle to the Ephesians, he had come to think of the whole Christian Body as a living Temple composed of individual personal temples — "each several building [i.e., temple] fitly framed together groweth into a holy Temple in the Lord for a habitation of God in the Spirit." It is difficult for us to pass in imagination from a temple as a structure of stone occupying space somewhere in a city to a human person who has become a revealing place for God and then to many such persons fused together through love and service to form one mighty corporate Temple which is God's new habitation. Just that is St. Paul's bold conception — the new Body composed of persons is to be the dwelling place and the revealing place of the Spirit, the organ of Christ's Life in the world.

— PC 138–39, 143–48

THE NEW SPIRIT AND THE NEW WORLD

There will always be among us so-called realists, conservative-minded persons, entrenched in the status quo, who insist that human nature is just "human nature." It cannot be changed. One might as well expect, these disciples of the Preacher in Ecclesiastes would say, to see figs growing on crabapple trees as to expect to see human instincts transformed from egoist urges into social and cooperative influences. "What has been is what will be, and there is nothing new under the sun." For a human dreamer to project a new kind of world and spin ideals out of his head is as absurd as for an amoeba to try to conjure up a paradise out of the slime of its mud puddle.

It may just possibly turn out that the "realist" is the "dreamer," that he is the one who is projecting, and not dealing with facts. Somehow the world has gone up and forward from the single-cell, amoeba-type of life to our complicated human type. And very much of the progress, at least in the last stages of advance, has been due to someone's power to forecast. Certain ideals have proved to be efficacious. They have been dynamic. They have worked. They have pulled groups of people forward. Not all ideals, of course, are constructive. Some are futile dreams. Ideals must be tested and sifted like other forces. But when the time is ripe for it and the mental climate is favorable, a forward-reaching ideal lifts like a magnetized giant crane. These cranes have a lifting arm charged with magnetic energy and they unload steel rails by mere contact. You see the heavy rail rise from its freight car and swing over to its new place without any grip or tie, with no hold but an invisible attraction.

These fresh lifting ideals emerge out of individual and social experience somewhat as mutations emerge in the biological series. These mutations may be just chance sports with no futurity, or they may be new forms that lift the entire order of life to higher levels. In any case they are new and unpredictable, and having come, they must forthwith stand the tests of struggle and survival. So, too, ideals arrive here in a world that did not expect them. They break in through some prophet-spirit, some leader, who has a vision for the next step in the forward march of the race. Usually, if the prophet is a real leader, he possesses a rare gift of sensitiveness to feel, like the migrating bird, the forward-pointing direction. He does not exactly create the ideal. It is truer to say that he discovers it. He feels the onward tendency of the age. He catches the vague hopes of his forerunners. He draws to a focus many unfulfilled aspirations and desires. He becomes the living organ of aims and purposes which till then have been abortive. He tries out his ideal and finds that it lifts others. It dynamizes kindred spirits. It produces faith. It organizes a group. It makes a center of energy. And, if conditions are right and the ideal is an efficacious one, before long a certain part of the human race has come up to a new level and has launched a new way of living, somewhat as the attraction of the moon lifts an immense plateau of the ocean, directly under it, twenty-five feet higher than the surrounding water. . . .

I have said enough, I hope, to make my main point clear. It is this, that the world progresses through the formation of an enlarging ideal of life, which in the first instance is the vision of a prophet. Then his vision dynamizes a group of disciples who are loyal to that ideal and it becomes the way of life and the driving force of a group or team of many members. And then if the ideal fits the higher needs of the race it slowly wins its way and becomes a dominant system of thought and action. Some of the purer and nobler aspects of the original ideal — some of the features which are "too" ideal for everyday human life — are likely to drop away, or be compromised and adjusted, as the circle of the group widens. But nevertheless large masses of men will in this manner be lifted to higher levels as the ideal wins its way and becomes a widespread principle of life and action.

The Quaker movement is historically one of these group-systems. At its heart and center there is a dominant ideal — a vision of a world that ought to be. It has been an attempt to

practice and to spread a spirit, a way of life, and to cultivate a
group dedicated to that aim. The phrase "a spirit" is, of course,
loose and vague. It needs to be interpreted. This group of people
is trying to demonstrate the fact that Christ's Galilean program
is a way of life which "works" better than any other one does.
Its essential aspects are: faith in God as Father, faith in man
as a potential son of God, and faith in the growing sway and
kingdom of God on earth; faith in the creative and conquering power of love as a method of life with our fellows; faith in
the attempt to understand men sympathetically; faith in an appeal to the higher diviner possibilities in men, and faith in the
final effect of the cooperative and self-giving spirit. This is, no
doubt, an optimistic program; so also was Christ's program of
life. There are, however, ugly opposing facts to be faced. There
is admittedly a sad amount of human wreckage. Thugs and ban-
dits are as much a reality in our world as are saints. Merciless
competition is in evidence. There are men, and women too, with
hard, fierce faces and with hard, pitiless hearts who think no
more of murdering a person in order to gain their ends than
most of us do of killing a mosquito that annoys us. The gentle,
trusting soul often enough has his trust and confidence abused
and frequently discovers that unscrupulous people take advan-
tage of the "easy mark." There are ages of struggle for existence
behind us and the fittest to survive have often been the strongest
and the best fighters. If the way of the transgressor is hard, it
would also seem to be true that the way of the soft and gentle
optimist is no less difficult to maintain.

I do not blink any of these facts, and the list of hard realities could run on to much greater length and still be true.
This is certainly not "the best possible world" — I can think
of a much better one — and if the word "optimist" is to be
taken in its superlative sense I am not one of that extreme type.
What I am contending for as a working principle is the faith

that the world *can be* remolded nearer to our hearts' desire, that we can rebuild the moral and spiritual world, and that we can do it by the cultivation of a new spirit, by the practice of a new way of life, and by loyalty to ideals of love, cooperation, and fellowship. The important question, as Phillips Brooks used to say, is whether, in our admittedly checkerboard world of black and white, the black squares are on a white background, or the white squares on a black background. It is a deep-seated Quaker faith that the permanent background is white, not black, and that the ultimate nature of the universe backs the aims that are true and the things that are good.

This method of faith in the remolding of the world will meet with defeats as well as with victories. Christ was allowed only three years of ministry, love, and service before He was hurried to the cross and His way of life condemned by the prevailing interests of the day. "Away with this man!" they cried. "Give us Barabbas; we can understand *his* methods!" Yes, but that cross did not terminate Christ's way of life. It proved to be one of its greatest energies and springs of power. It laid a spell on men's hearts. It won the soul of a thief and bandit who was dying within sight of it. It powerfully moved the centurion who beheld it. It conquered the young scholar from Tarsus and it became his battle cry: "I will not glory in anything save the Cross of Christ." It brought the greatest Carthaginian that ever lived, Augustine of Hippo, to this way of life. It was the inspiration and power in the life of that poor little man of Assisi, as it is today in the life and work of Gandhi. There has been no other conqueror to be compared with the Galilean. "Art thou a king?" Pilate asked, and the bold answer came: "To this end was I born and for this cause came I into the world that I might bear witness to the truth." He has been ruling and conquering ever since Pilate yielded and pronounced his sentence. Who knows whether defeat may not sometimes be more important than so-called victories? Are "lost causes" really lost? In any case, we need not be disturbed by the fact that the world is organized on a basis of strength, force and power, and that the "new way" can win only by slow stages and through defeats and pain and suffering. All we need to know at present is that the new way is the right way and that the universe is so constructed that in the end this new way can prevail....

The Quakers have never assumed that the new world was to be built by miracle or that it would be a light and easy matter to swing over from the way of force to the way of love. They have suffered and agonized through many wars in which they could not take part. They have endured the despoiling of goods, the hostile cry of hate, and sometimes even the loss of life, because they would not share in the old way of force and carnage. Their position has often appeared absurd. They seem to ignore facts. It looks as though they were living in a fool's paradise and nursing an insane dream. "Would you let a thug kill your wife, burn your house, carry off your goods, and do nothing to restrain him?" The problem of how to deal with the thug offers no real parallel to the methods of war. Nations are not thugs. They are bodies of intelligent people. Their claims and causes and charges are either just or unjust. They would practically never push their claims, causes, and charges to extreme issue if they were met with kindness, intelligence, and wisdom by the nation with whom they are in dispute. In any case, fighting will not settle whether the claims were just or unjust. It will only settle which nation can mobilize and handle its fighting forces and its economic forces the better. When the war ends, it will be found that there was an equal amount of thuggery practiced on both sides, that terrible things were done to force the final victory. Multitudes of innocent persons will have suffered. The little children of the two countries will be the main victims. Lands will be made desolate. Social progress will be arrested.

The poor will be swamped with taxes for an entire generation. The mutilated men will drag out a broken life to the end of their days. A large part of the "facts" used to arouse patriotism and to stir the fervor and the fierceness of the fighting spirit will be discovered to have been propaganda. And yet not one single thing will have been done to determine where right or justice or truth lay in the issues involved.

In view of these things, Friends are pledged to another way of life. They will not ally themselves to the way of war, nor to its methods or its deeds. It is difficult, of course, to live in a world *which is being made.* We build our cities on strata of the earth which may without a moment's warning break, slip, tilt, quake, and shake the entire city down into a heap of ruins. These catastrophes used to be attributed to God; we now see that it is a human risk which we ourselves take when we construct a city on a strip of the earth's crust which is only partly finished. Still less finished is man himself, and least of all the social fabric upon which we must build our systems and our ideals. We are still in the infancy of the race. The diseases of childhood are not all over. The moods and passions of unripe years occasionally sweep in and disturb the household. It is bound to be difficult trying to live by ideals for which the slowly maturing world is not quite ready. But it is the price that must be paid for prophetic vision and it is a risk well worth taking.

The alternative would be to refuse to follow any vision of life which ran ahead of the settled practice of society, to decline to deviate from the customs and habits of one's time and to wait for the better conditions of life until they emerge from the sky, or peradventure come by the sheer drive of evolution, or until by some happy chance the race all together decides to leap to a new height. The alternative is a vain hope. Social progress is not inevitable. It is not like the escalator, the moving staircase, which goes steadily on and carries the climber upward whether he walks or not. There is an inherent risk attaching to our social partnerships. We cannot be persons without being woven into a social group, and, alas, the group to which we belong is not on an escalator. If it goes upwards, it will be because some of us who belong to it take the risk of practicing a forward-looking vision; because we are ready to make hard sacrifices for a truth that has broken in on our souls; because we are done with the old pettifogging methods in vogue and take the chances and the penalties of trying an advance.

But these visions of advance must not be just pious aspirations, subjects for drawing room conversation when we have exhausted the possibilities of the weather, nor must they be mere propaganda topics for lecture halls and forums. Visions of advance are things to be done, not to be easily talked about. They are ways of living, not dreams of a sleeper. The Quakers have been primarily doers. They believe strongly in the laboratory method. They try their experiment and then proceed to interpret it. The words, the talk, come after the deeds. It is Quaker faith that war can be eliminated only by a way of life that first eliminates hate, greed, fear, jealousy, rivalry, injustice, misunderstanding, misjudging, and overreaching. But so long as that faith is only an untested theory, it is nothing but a pious hope. The Quaker has endeavored to try it, to make an experiment with it, in the interwoven tissues of social life. Having started this experiment in peace times, he cannot give it up and resort to the methods of hate and fear as soon as war is declared. He believes that it is a matter of a good deal of importance to have a body of people, even though it may be a small body, who will not surrender their ideal — their vision of advance — even in the face of the earthquake and the broken strata. It is worth something to have the lighted torch held high, when others have allowed the swirl of the storm to blow theirs out.

The only way the new kind of world will eventually come will be through the persistence, the patience, and the unyielding faith of those who will not surrender, nor compromise, nor mistake expediency for truth. . . . It is, of course, much more than a question of war and peace between nations. The method which I am presenting — the new spirit — applies to all the affairs of life. We cannot very well get our new world of international relations until we find out how to eliminate the catastrophes of war. We must somehow make our house secure against these periodic earthquakes, but it is no less important to reorganize, on the same principle, our business operations, our family life, our political systems, and our ecclesiastical fellowships. Hates and fears and rivalries are not confined to the international sphere. The wastes which our present civilization entails are not limited to periods of war. We waste the precious raw material of the earth all the time. Our haste and rivalry, our fear that somebody will get ahead of us in exploiting the rich deposits in the soil of the earth are squandering the limited stock of supplies, which ought to be handled with the utmost care and conserved for those who will come after us. But much more serious is the waste of human life. We exploit men and women and children as well as coal and oil. We build our cities for the ease and convenience of commerce, not for the promotion of life and happiness. The slum is an outrage against humanity. The narrow, treeless streets, without gardens and breathing spaces for the play of children, are marks of selfishness, ignorance, and stupidity. The mills and factories and mines, where labor is massed, where initiative and creative qualities are eliminated, where a person is largely reduced to a mechanistic tool, involve a large sum total both of blunders and sins against palpitating human beings whom God has made.

We are all part of it and we are all responsible for the evil conditions, and we shall never have a new world here until we wake up and want it and are ready to pay the high price which it will cost. There is once more no escalator for this. It will come only as we make experiments with another way of living.... It means once more the practice of a new spirit rather than the abstract formulation of a new theory of society. It means the brave adoption of a new way of living. It involves greater simplicity of life, more sacrifices, more love and sympathy, less selfishness and rivalry....

Our real problem is the formation of the right spirit. No changes in the proportions of wealth and poverty would be adequate, though they might produce favoring conditions. No political reorganizations would work the miracle. Sooner or later we must learn to love and trust one another. We must form the habit of sharing and cooperating. We must be as ready to sacrifice as we now are to compete. There is no substitute for the new spirit and the new way of life. We shall need experts, wise guides, persons who have clear insight and sound wisdom, but with experts or no experts, we shall never get our happy, joyous, peaceful world until we learn to love and understand and share and become brothers to one another, because we are children of a common Father.   —FP 160–62, 165–76

L'Envoi

Breaking through Fog

I have recently been on a sea trip, much of the time enveloped in
a thick fog. The range of visibility was extremely short. The ship
crept along cautiously, feeling its way and sounding the foghorn
at frequent intervals. The horn had no note of joy or triumph. It
was a sound only of fear and warning. Every other ship in the
neighborhood was a menace and each ship in turn was afraid
of us. But while the fog lasted our ship was concerned almost
wholly for its own safety. The noises it made were for its own
protection, and the lower the visibility dropped the more wor-
ried everyone became for the safety of the ship to which he had
committed his destiny.

The first thing that impressed me as we lived in the fog was
the severe limitations which it imposed upon our life. There
was no sky over us, no horizon, no color, no beauty, no proper
world. If we were always doomed to live in a fog-bound world
we should never know that a sun existed or a moon or the stars.
There would be no astronomy. We could only guess at what
caused the variations of light and darkness. We should vaguely
surmise that there must be some power out beyond the veil of
fog, that shifted the scenes of day and night. But no one could

dream of the glory of sunrise and sunset, nor would there be any hint of the sublimity and wonder of the stars.

The slightest change in the atmosphere conditions of our world would lodge us permanently in a low visibility world like that. The raindrop which dispels the fog can form only where there is an infinitesimal particle present, around which as a tiny nucleus the moisture condenses into the rain globule, which then falls by its own weight. In perfectly pure air there could be no rain, as also there would be no color and no dome of sky. At sea it is the presence in the air of tiny fragments of salt crystals that form the nucleus for the formation of raindrops and thus serve for the clarification of the air by the deposit of moisture.

Some day, perhaps not far distant, it will almost certainly be possible by artificial means to dispel fog and to open a path of light in front of ships. Successful experiments have already been made in removing fog from small areas, but the process is expensive and the mechanism too cumbersome to be practical. Yet it may assuredly be predicted that the human mind will in the course of time find a way to conquer this obstacle to safety on the sea and in the air. When that time comes the ship will be able to protect itself, not by discordant and disturbing noises, but by the projection of a path of light which will give help and guidance to all nearby ships as well as safety to itself.

But this condition of low visibility at sea may very well become a parable of the spiritual climate through which we have been passing. Our visibility has plainly enough been running low. There has been a loss of sky and stars, and a very low visibility for any realities beyond the near ones. One could vaguely guess that there must be more than was revealed here within the enveloping veils of time and space, but in spite of the dim guess life has remained shut in, contracted, and painfully limited both in upward reach and in stretch of horizon. Instead of trying to dissipate the mental fog and clear away the veils, we have been busy with our small concerns for self-safety and security, and with attempts to make great noises of warning and intimations of menace to all who are in the path of our onward speed.

The time has come for the projection of a path of light that will clear away the fog, open up the sky, rediscover the stars, and reveal to awakened observers that there is a celestial luminary which our self-made fogs have too long concealed from us. The greatest fog-dispelling contrivance that has ever been found for crises like this one is a new burst of moral enthusiasm, the driving energy of spiritual passion. We have been drifting about in the mists of cynicism and distrust, blowing our foghorn of despair and danger. Enthusiasm cannot, of course, be pumped up and shot out of a spigot. Moral passion is not something that can be commandeered at need. Nor shall we pass from dense fog to open sky by a lift of our own bootstraps, or, to change the figure, by a puff of our own breath on our sails.

I obviously omitted an important factor when I spoke of projects for dispelling fog by human effort. They may work eventually within a very limited area. In any case they show man's unconquerable spirit. But, after all, "the important factor" is the cosmic drive against the fog, which effects what man with all his powers could never do. The sun fights it from above. The shifts of temperature doom it. The currents of air and sea settle its fate. The tiny crystals of salt from the spray carry it away in little globules of rain. A few moments ago we were immersed in it and now the blue sky is over us. The horizon is a perfect circle, the air is as clear and bright as the stones in the walls of the New Jerusalem. The cosmic drive has accomplished what no enginery of man could have done.

It is so, too, with this other fog which besets us and envelops us round. Our own efforts are all to the good. Our moral enthusiasms are noble, our spiritual passions count for something. But the best of it all is, there is cosmic free grace working for us. A realm of a higher order is over and around us. The celestial luminary of that realm, Who is the source and fountain of life, is forever breaking through the veils and working for us even when we fail to see His light and love. Our best line of action and cooperation is to become quick and acute to note His revelations. What we need most just now is to discover or rediscover where He has broken in and manifested the grace by which we can conquer and dispel the darkness.   — TS 211–15